DAREDEVILS AND DESPERADOES

20 Stories from British History

Geraldine McCaughrean

Illustrated by Richard Brassey

Galaxy

CHIVERS PRESS
BATH

First published 2002
by
Orion Children's Books
This Large Print edition published by
Chivers Press
by arrangement with
Orion Children's Books
2003

ISBN 0 7540 7845 0

The stories in this volume were originally
published as part of *Britannia: 100 Great
Stories from British History*, first published by
Orion Children's Books in 1999.

British Library Cataloguing in Publication Data

McCaughrean, Geraldine
    Devils and desperadoes.—Large print ed.
    1. Legends—Juvenile fiction 2. Mythology, British—
Juvenile fiction 3. Children's stories, English 4. Large
type books 5. Great Britain—History—Juvenile fiction
I. Title II. Brassey, Richard
823. 9'14[J]

ISBN 0-7540-7845-0

Printed and bound in Great Britain by
BOOKCRAFT, Midsomer Norton, Somerset

For Alice

CONTENTS

INTRODUCTION

Rebellion, crime and war figure time and again in this volume. Dredging itself up out of a hundred years of war and civil strife, Britain at last reached the glory years of the Tudors. Ordinary people began finding their voice, quarrelling about religion, splitting into factions, growing richer. Scotland was at loggerheads with England. Politics was the sport of the hour.

And where there are politicians there are always lies. So watch out for the liars and opportunists among the heroes, explorers and magnificos.

THE GARTER

1348

The dancers promenaded up and down, forming circles, forming lines, interweaving like the threads of the silken banners overhead. Surrounded by the heraldry of fifty ancient families and the crested helmets of warrior knights, the dancers themselves formed a kind of heraldry, bright with colours and chivalric splendour.

Then the Countess of Salisbury's garter slipped, slid down and came off altogether, to lie on the marble floor. Nobody could miss it. A page tittered. A gossip pointed. And the music ended just as King Edward saw it too.

Splendid in a quartered doublet of silk-lined velvet, he made a low sweep of his hand, a flourishing bow to his dancing partner, and his fingers scooped up the offending garter.

The countess flushed a vivid red. The silk stocking, which the garter had been holding up, wrinkled unceremoniously round her ankle. Was the King going to make some coarse joke? Humiliate her in front of her friends and inferiors? Would this model prince really do such a thing?

Edward pointed a toe and slipped his own foot through the garter, sliding it up as far as it would go round his manly calf. The crowd did not know if it was a joke. Two or three nervous giggles erupted from the courtiers. King Edward, turning his leg this way and that, heel in, heel out, looked up sharply. 'Shame on him whose thoughts are shameful!' he said. *'Honi soit qui mal y pense.'*

It was the kind of slogan noble houses were adopting the length and breadth of Europe, in the great race to invent a new, more civilized nobility: devices, mottoes, heraldic beasts, liveries, crests and honours. Some flattering duke jotted down the King's words in a commonplace book. The music struck up again and the countess, still pink with a mixture of

embarrassment and pleasure, joined fingertips with the King once more. The slow, prancing geometry of the next dance began.

The lady's garter flashed and flickered on the King's calf—elevated now to the status of colours on the lance-point of a jousting chevalier. By the end of the dance the King had pursued his chivalrous thought still further. Again he thrust forward his leg and declared: 'Only the greatest in the land shall wear such a garter! Let it be awarded only to my most favoured subjects! Only the most esteemed and chivalrous men in the kingdom will share with me this honour, this privilege of wearing . . . *the Garter!*'

And so the Order of the Garter began—at a time when English pride was at its height, when it lay in the power of a king to grant everlasting glory.

The order of the Garter is the oldest surviving order of Chivalry in Europe and was invented in the wake of an English victory in the Hundred Years War with France. Chivalry was reshaping the very nature of bravery, virtue and love. The story is cast into doubt by another in which Edward gave the signal for a victorious battle charge by waving his own blue garter. But whatever the origin of the award, it is now worn by only twenty-four honoured recipients (plus royal and

overseas VIPs) at any one time, and only when one dies is another appointed to this most prestigious circle of all.

DICK WHITTINGTON

1358–1423

 Once upon a time, a poor boy called Dick lived in a village in the middle of nowhere. He had no mother or father to feed or clothe him, no future, so it seemed. 'You should go to London!' said a neighbour. 'They say the streets there are paved with gold!'

So Dick set off to walk, thinking London must be just over the hill. A hundred hills later, he found himself in narrow streets, among high houses and the shouts and bustle of London. His poor sore feet found no golden pavements to walk on—not so much as a golden pebble. And his stomach was empty.

He got work scraping pots in the kitchen of Captain Fitz-Warren, a rich merchant. Though Dick could eat the scrapings, the cook was a cruel bully.

7

Dick slept in an attic so overrun with mice that with his first sixpence he bought a cat. That cat was a good friend to Dick, and he came to love it . . . almost as much as he came to love Captain Fitz-Warren's daughter, Alice. Sweet, kind, beautiful Alice. 'If I weren't me and you weren't you, I would marry you one day!' he used to say.

'Who knows what you might be one day,' Alice would say in reply.

But the cook's cruelties were too much for Dick to bear, and one very early morning he and his cat ran away. He might have walked all the way home, had he not stopped to rest on a milestone at Holloway. Across the fields came the distant ringing of Bow Bells in Cheapside—a familiar enough

sound—except that today he seemed to hear words among the clamour: 'Turn again, Whittington, thrice Lord Mayor of London!'

At once, Dick ran back the way he had come, and was busy scrubbing the kitchen floor before the cook even woke.

That day the house was all at sixes and sevens. Captain Fitz-Warren was setting sail. All kinds of people had invested in his voyage, hoping for huge profits when the merchant sold his cargo in distant parts. 'Why not invest something yourself, Dick?' asked the merchant.

'Me? But I have nothing, sir,' said Dick.

'You have that cat of yours! I need a cat to keep down the rats on board my ship.'

Dick did not want to be parted from his friend, but at the last moment, he agreed.

Disaster! Captain Fitz-Warren's ship ran aground on the shores of a country where no one wanted or needed his valuable cargo. The caliph there had everything a man could desire: gems and silk, sherbet and oysters, palace walls clad in beaten gold.

One thing more the caliph had. Rats. His realm, his palace, even his throne-room swarmed with rats, because there were no cats in the whole land. When Puss saw the rats, he slew them by the dozen, by the tens of dozen, while the caliph watched in wonder. 'For this cat I will pay three sacks of diamonds!' he declared.

Dick's fortune was made. With the proceeds, he became a respected London merchant and before long he was elected Lord Mayor of London —not once but three times. Bow Bells rang once again for Dick Whittington—on the day he married Alice Fitz-Warren.

Sir William Whittington of Gloucestershire had three sons but, when the youngest was still a baby, he was outlawed. The two older brothers sent Dick to London to be apprenticed to a distant relation, Sir Ivo Fitzwaryn. Sir Ivo was a mercer—a dealer in fabrics—and Dick's first job, at thirteen, was to stand outside his master's shop shouting, to attract customers. 'What d'ye lack? What d'ye lack?'

From early morning till Bow Bells rang at eight, Dick learned his trade.

They were eventful times. He saw John Wycliffe tried for heresy, saw Wat Tyler's rebels come flooding over London Bridge, saw the plague carry off 30,000 people in a single year.

They were fashionable times, too— times when the rich spent lavishly on clothes. There was no better time to be a mercer. The London mercers had money to spare, so became the bankers of the day as well, growing even richer from lending money.

By the age of twenty-nine Richard Whittington had £10 of his own to invest. At thirty-five he was an alderman and sheriff. King Richard II appointed him Mayor of London (there was no Lord Mayor then). His fellow Londoners re-elected him time after time.

Mayor Whittington invented street lighting, commanding every citizen to hang a lantern outside his door at night. He invented the public drinking

fountain, too. He was the terror of dishonest tradesmen, prosecuting those who gave short measure, watered beer, overcharged or sold shoddy goods. He rebuilt his parish church, built almshouses for the poor, began a vast library . . . and lent King Henry V £60,000 towards the cost of fighting a war in France.

He entertained Henry and his new bride, Princess Catherine of France, to a feast more splendid than any ever seen before, warming the banqueting hall with three blazing fires of costly cedarwood and cinnamon. Queen Catherine clapped her hands in delight at such sweet-smelling, extravagant fires.

'Ah, but I shall feed them with something more costly still than cedarwood!' declared Sir Richard, and promptly tossed into the fire all record of moneys he had lent King Henry. 'Thus do I acquit your Highness of a debt of £60,000,' he said.

Henry was staggered. 'Never had a prince such a subject!' he cried.

'Never had a subject such a prince,' said Whittington with a gracious bow.

Whittington *did* marry his employer's daughter, Alice. But they had no children. So when the great man died a widower, his immense wealth was bequeathed to London—to rebuild Newgate Prison, to restore St Bart's Hospital, to put windows in the Guildhall, to found a college . . . and his library of books was given to the Greyfriars. He had many 'cats' (for the word means a cargo-carrying sailing boat); but as to the furry kind—well, they leave no pawprints on the pages of history.

SAY 'BREAD AND CHEESE'

1381

'When Adam delved and Eve span, who was then the gentleman?' John Ball asked the question in market squares all over Kent, and no one could answer him. Everybody is descended from Adam and Eve. So how come some people have become knights and barons, the rest starving serfs, taxed and oppressed by their so-called 'betters'? Ball was a 'Lollard'. He wanted to end the feudal system. The people of Kent were eager to help him.

At Dartford, the cry was taken up by Walter the Tiler (or Wat Tyler).

Unlike Ball (an educated priest with strong religious beliefs), Tyler was a hooligan and a murderer. But the people followed him, like children following the Pied Piper. Joining forces with John Ball and a thatcher named Jack Straw, Tyler began to march towards London trailing behind him a growing army of protesters. Some just wanted to tell the young King their grievances; some wanted to bring down the old order, some simply a chance to pillage the city and cut a few throats.

Out of other counties came other columns of marchers. The citizens of London, faced with this flood of angry rebels, slammed the gates of London Bridge, to keep them out.

'Tell them to gather on the Thames shore at Rotherhithe on Thursday, and I will speak to them,' said King Richard.

He was only fifteen, but appeared calm as he and a company of barons sailed down-river to meet the rebels. At the sight of him, the huge crowd on the bank raised a noise 'like all the devils in hell', and surged towards the river. It was impossible to judge their mood. 'Don't go ashore, your Majesty!' the barons begged. 'It's too dangerous!'

So the boy-king stood up in the prow of the barge. 'What do you wish?' he shouted.

'Come ashore, and we'll tell you!' the

mob shouted back.

The Earl of Salisbury stood up, rocking the boat. 'Gentlemen, you are not properly dressed for conversation with a king!' As the barge pulled out again into mid-stream, the crowd muttered angrily, and headed for London. Finding the gates of London Bridge shut, they threatened to burn down the suburbs and take the city by storm.

Could they be fought off? The Lord Mayor was doubtful. The City itself was full of rebel sympathizers—maybe as many as 30,000 living *inside* the gates might rise up, too, if it came to a battle. Slowly, creakingly, the gates were swung open, and the mob surged across —hundreds of hungry men. Sooner than be plundered of everything, grocers and bakers hurried into the street to distribute food.

A mob is a mindless, savage beast. This one went through the city looting, setting fire to the homes of lawyers, courtiers and churchmen. They burned down the Savoy Palace, the house of the Knights Hospitallers and the

Marshalsea Prison. It was a night for
settling old scores. Wat Tyler searched
out an old employer who had crossed
him once, and hacked off his head.

His power-crazed army grabbed
people in the street, shaking them by

the throat and screaming: 'Say "bread and cheese!"' When times are hard, the poor and the ignorant always blame foreigners for their troubles. Any trace of a foreign accent and they killed their victim. 'Say "bread and cheese!"'

'Brod unt cheess.'

'Kill him! Kill the foreigner!'

Sixty-two innocent Flemish citizens were murdered that night for the crime of speaking with an accent. Meanwhile, inside the Tower of London, Richard II and his Council discussed the best way to deal with the revolt.

'When they're all drunk or asleep, we can go out and kill them like flies!' it was suggested. 'Not one in ten has a weapon, and we can muster—what?—800 armed men!'

But the Earl of Salisbury shook his head. The mob must be appeased, soothed with kind words. 'If we should begin to kill them, and not go through with it, it will be all over with us and our heirs. England will become a desert.'

So Richard sent word telling the rebels to meet him at Mile End meadow where he would discuss their demands.

Only half the mob believed him. The rest were too busy cutting throats. Waiting till the gates of the Tower were opened and the King's party gone, Ball and Tyler and Straw sped across the drawbridge, scouring the maze of apartments and staircases for the people they hated most. They slashed the bed of the Princess of Wales. They beheaded the Archbishop of Canterbury, killed a prior, a friar and a sergeant-at-arms, and mounted their heads on poles to decorate London Bridge. Then on to Mile End meadow.

Tens of thousands of peasants from every county in England confronted Richard as he rode out to speak with the leaders of the Peasants' Revolt. Some of his pages and courtiers were so scared that they turned their horses and galloped away, abandoning the young King. But his nerve held.

'My good people. What is it you want and what do you wish to say to me?'

'We want you to make us free for ever,' said a man nearby.

'I grant your wish,' said Richard.

Just like that. An end to serfdom. An end to one man 'owning' another.

It took the wind out of their sails. It defused the moment. It turned the mob back into a dignified assembly of loyal subjects. 'Go home now,' said Richard. 'Leave two men behind from every village, and I will have letters written, sealed with my seal, for them to carry home. I shall send my banners, too, as proof that you have my authority.'

Thirty secretaries were summoned to write those precious letters, and as each one was sealed and delivered, large numbers of protesters turned for home, saying, 'All's well. We have what we wanted.'

Not Wat Tyler. Not Jack Straw. Not John Ball, nor thousands of others. They had the City of London at their mercy, and were not going to leave till it was stripped bare. Still more peasants were converging on London, and the looters had no wish to share their plunder with newcomers.

Almost by chance, King Richard and sixty outriders came face-to-face with the vast, drunken mob at Smithfield. Fresh in Richard's mind were the horrors he had found at the Tower—those four headless bodies, the blood, the trail of destruction leading from room to room. And yet the words of the Earl of Salisbury were still ringing in his ears: '. . . England will become a desert.'

When he recognized the King, Tyler gave a terse laugh and fumbled for his stirrup, to mount. He was keyed-up, drunk on stolen wine and lack of sleep. 'Stay here. Don't stir until I give you a signal. When I make this sign, come forward and kill everyone except the King. He's young and we can do with him what we please.'

Then he rode forward—so impetuously that his horse ran its nose into Richard's. 'King,' he blurted out, 'do you see all those men there? They are all under my command and have sworn to do whatever I shall order.' He wanted the King's letters, he said—would not leave London without them in his hand.

'That is what has been ordered. They will be delivered as fast as they can be written,' the fifteen-year-old King answered calmly.

But Tyler was hysterical, overwrought, wanting to prove what power he wielded. 'Give me your dagger!' he told the King's squire. The squire refused, but Richard told him to give it up. 'Now your sword!' demanded Tyler. The squire refused.

The Mayor blustered: 'How dare you behave thus in the presence of the King!'

Richard remembered those four headless bodies, all that blood. 'Lay hands on him!'

A sword struck Tyler so hard on the head that he fell. The royal party milled around, their horses blocking the crowd's view. A squire dismounted and finished Wat Tyler where he lay. Messengers rode off to the city for reinforcements.

Then the body was spotted. 'They have killed our captain! Let's kill the whole pack of them!' The mob drew a single breath. Arrows were laid to ash-wood bows, and the crowd began to move, like volcanic lava, bubbling, seething. What happened in the next few seconds would decide the fate of everyone there.

'No one follow me!' said King Richard, and urged his horse towards the furious crowd. Rising in his stirrups, he yelled: 'Gentlemen! What are you about? You shall have no other captain but me. I am your King!'

It was a startling gesture from a boy of his age. Thousands drew back from the brink. Some hotheads wanted to cut down the King, but hesitated, uncertain.

That hesitation gave time for several thousand armed men to ride, pell-mell, out of London, and reinforce King and court.

John Ball and Jack Straw crept away, hoping to hide.

'Let's charge, and kill them where they stand!' urged one of Richard's knights, but the King would not hear of it. There was no need. The balance of power had changed. King Richard was demanding the return of his banners, the handing back of his letters. And the people were passing them forward—banners and letters—giving up their passports to freedom.

In front of their eyes, Richard tore up the letters, crushed the waxy seals, and they stood and watched him do it—docile, cowed, leaderless. Like sheep they scattered. Like sheepdogs at their heels, new proclamations chased them out of town. Anyone not resident in London one year or more was to be gone by Sunday or lose his head.

As they streamed over London Bridge, three severed heads grinned down at them from the top of poles: not the archbishop nor the prior nor the sergeant-at-arms, but Wat Tyler, Jack Straw and John Ball. On the various roads to London, thousands of peasants still thronging to join in the Peasant's Revolt heard that it was over—and turned back.

Who was in the wrong? Tyler and his murderous louts? The King and Parliament, with their broken promises? After the peasants returned home, every letter was revoked, every charter withdrawn. Even more hardships were heaped on the peasants. Large crowds were forbidden to gather. Richard II imposed his authority by marching around the country with an army of 40,000 men. The nobles were no more ready to set serfs free than to give away

their own knives and forks. Property is property, after all.

In some regions, the Peasants' Revolt was not so easily snuffed out. There were risings all over the country, and nobles shut themselves up in their castles and trembled. But order was gradually restored by the usual means: battles, trials, beheadings; in Essex, 500 peasants were killed.

'A LITTLE TOUCH OF HARRY IN THE NIGHT'

(Shakespeare, *Henry V*)

1415

From the French camp floated the noise of blacksmiths hammering home rivets, a minstrel singing, men laughing; banners of red-and-yellow light. But within the English camp there was hardly a sound, hardly a light showing. Six thousand exhausted men had walked through teeming rain 260 miles from Harfleur with too little to eat and disease dogging them every step of the way. In the morning they would have to confront the army barring their road to Calais and escape. And the well-equipped French outnumbered them four-to-one. There did not seem much to sing about, as the rain teemed and the dark pressed suffocatingly close.

'Who goes there?' The sentries were jumpy.

'Friend.'

'Whose regiment?'

'Sir Thomas Erpingham's.' The cloaked figure moved closer, hood pulled forward against the filthy weather. The sentry let him pass and join a group of men sitting round a damp little fire.

'It's all right for the King,' one was saying. 'He wants to win the throne of France, so we have to come here and die.'

'Is that how you see it?' said the hooded stranger equably. He took a sip of ale, before passing his tankard on round the group. 'I would have thought the King had a heavy burden to carry. He's the father of his men. He has to provide for them, pray for them, look after them . . . All those wives and children depending on him to bring home their menfolk—that's a terrible responsibility for any man.'

'Yeah, but tomorrow he'll be up there on his big horse on top of a hill somewhere, watching us get trampled by the French cavalry.'

'Oh, why? Was Harfleur like that?'

Another answered instead. 'No! No, at Harfleur, Harry was right there at our elbow, fighting like a demon!'

'Yeah, you can say that for the saucy rogue,' admitted a sergeant grudgingly. 'Harry's not afraid to get his hands dirty.'

They turned to speak more, but the stranger was moving away. For a second the firelight caught his face and the sergeant's hand shot out and gripped the man alongside him. 'Oh no! You know who that was, don't you? You know what I just done? I only went and called the King of England a saucy rogue to his face!'

Henry walked on, moving between the dim red circles of dying campfires like a meteor through the dimness of space, calling out greetings to those he knew by name. Some recognized him, even bare-headed and without his surcoat of leopards and lilies. The King was a tall, erect figure, with a long, straight nose and strong jawline. His voice was sometimes soft and soothing, sometimes bright and laughing, depending on the nature and needs of his men. He played dice with some, exchanged memories with others, broke bread with them, listened to their jokes. He did not sleep that night, but the following morning his men were less weary because of it.

Only then did he begin to speak of glory.

His sword was drawn as he spoke, rallying them, encouraging them, praising their valour and skill as warriors. The men farthest off craned to catch every last word. Henry invited all those who wanted to leave, to go with his blessing—but warned them that they would miss out on the glory, miss out on being part of the greatest battle ever fought. No one got up to leave. When he had finished, there was no more talk of dying under French hooves, no more lolling in the mud nursing belly aches and fear. Henry had his men mustered and ready while the French were still quarrelling about who would lead the charge.

So sure of victory were the swaggering French knights, that they bragged to one another: 'I shall capture the English banner!'

'I shall take a thousand prisoners!'

'They haven't above 900 men-at-arms! The rest are nothing but poxy archers!'

Their horses pranced and capered under them, so unruly that their commander could not apply his battle plan. They even managed to trap 3,000 of their own crossbowmen behind them, leaving them unable to fire on the enemy for fear of hitting French knights.

At mid-morning, with a shout from Henry of, 'Banners advance! In the name of Jesus, Mary and St George!' and with a blare of trumpets, the English trudged a half mile towards the enemy. When the French banners were just within range of the archers' arrows, the English halted and sank long, sharpened stakes into the sodden ground, points outward.

With a single unearthly note, the bowstrings of the English longbowmen loosed a swarm of arrows, blackening the sky. Death fell on the French like a plague of locusts.

Enraged by such unexpected casualties, 1,000 knights spurred their lumbering great horses into a charge. But the ground in front of them was boggy, and the English archers could fire off twelve arrows a minute— metre-long arrows whose tips could pierce armour. By the time the French cavalry reached the longbowmen, 850 out of 1,000 were dead. The survivors rode on to the wooden stakes, or were pulled from their saddles and done to death by the archers. Riderless horses and fleeing French knights turned and galloped back the way they had come— trampling their own foot-soldiers.

The first line of French infantry finally surged up. But they were so tightly massed that they had no room to swing their weapons. They could only mill about, gasping for breath. The English archers threw down their bows and fell on them with swords and axes. Unaware of the disaster at the front, more French men-at-arms came marching up from behind. The first line, now trapped, could neither advance nor retreat. More Frenchmen died of being crushed, than of wounds inflicted by the English.

The aristocratic knights, in their heavy, ornate armour lay in the mud, helpless to get to their feet, trampled by horses and running feet, drowning in mud. In three hours, 10,000 Frenchmen died—half of all the noblemen in France were either killed or captured.

The cost to the English was a mere one hundred men.

King Henry V, frivolous and unpromising as a young man, changed completely after his coronation in 1413, into a sober statesman. He believed so fervently in his claim to the French throne that he pawned the Crown jewels to fund a war, and borrowed hugely from such people as Dick Whittington (see page 7). By tireless warring, by the astounding victory at Agincourt and by marrying Catherine, daughter of the mad old King of France, he secured both England and France for his son.

Undoubtedly, English chroniclers of the battle exaggerated the difference in casualty figures. But the events recounted here are not simply some patriotic invention of Shakespeare's. His play *Henry V* (1599) was based on 'fact'—the chronicles of Hall and Holinshed. Henry V, king for only nine glorious years, was dead at the age of thirty-four.

'HANG ON THE BELL, NELLY!'

1460

'And this be the sentence of this court; that you be taken from this place and, at the sounding of the curfew bell, hanged by the neck until you are dead. And may God have mercy on your soul.'

The young man standing between his guards sagged a little at the knees, and a young woman in the court cried out, '*No!*' But the judge did not so much as look up. He had passed the death sentence so often before. In these days of war, death was commonplace.

This was the time of the Wars of the Roses. The young man—Neville Audeley—was a Lancastrian. In attempting to visit his sweetheart, Nell, he had been unlucky enough to fall into the hands of Yorkist troops. His only crime was to be on the wrong side in the wrong place, during an endlessly bloody civil war which had torn apart

39

families, and pitted neighbours and towns against one another. Once, Neville had given Nell roses, but all she had left now were the thorns embedded deep in her heart.

There was hope, even so. Neville was the nephew of the Earl of Warwick, and his uncle had influence. A word at court, a favour owing, and the earl might just win a reprieve for his nephew. But court was far off in London, and there was so little time! To Neville, gripping the bars of his prison cell, it seemed that the sun was crossing the sky with the speed of a cannonball, bringing his death hurtling towards him.

'Time to go,' said his gaoler, jangling the keys in the lock.

'But my reprieve! What of a reprieve?'

'What of it? If it comes after curfew, they may paste it on your tombstone.' He tied Neville's hands and led him down a dank stone passageway.

The day outside was already grey with age. There were a few towns-people still on the streets, despite the closeness of curfew. They would have to hurry home to put out their fires while the bell tolled . . . while Neville kicked out his life to the sound of St Peter's church bell. I shall never hear the last stroke of that curfew bell, he thought to himself, as he set his foot on the bottom rung of the gallows ladder.

He searched among the crowd for Nell, but to his utter dismay she was not there. Where was she, his 'little Nell'? Where was her sweet, encouraging face? It would have lent him such courage to catch one last glimpse of her. With her there, he thought he might at least have put on a show of bravery.

'For shame!' someone yelled. 'He's only a boy! Hold off, hangman. There'll be a reprieve come for sure! He's Nelly Heriot's sweetheart! He's only a lad!'

But the hangman worked to the letter of the law, and the law said that Audeley must die on the first stroke of curfew. The belltower of St Peter's cast its shadow across the square, dwarfing the town gibbet. The bellringer stepped

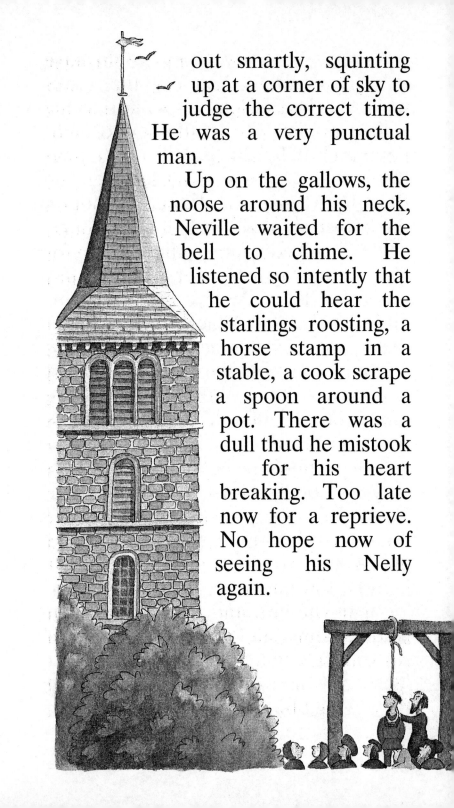

out smartly, squinting up at a corner of sky to judge the correct time. He was a very punctual man.

Up on the gallows, the noose around his neck, Neville waited for the bell to chime. He listened so intently that he could hear the starlings roosting, a horse stamp in a stable, a cook scrape a spoon around a pot. There was a dull thud he mistook for his heart breaking. Too late now for a reprieve. No hope now of seeing his Nelly again.

Inside St Peter's, the bellringer tugged again on the rope, but again there was no sound. He swung his whole body weight on the rope's end, but it was as if the bell had been struck dumb. Had frost broken off the clapper? Had the rope become entangled in the rafters? He pulled with a will—strong, rhythmic heaves: nothing but silence throbbed out into the darkening sky.

Beneath the gallows, the crowd began to stir restlessly. Surely the curfew should have rung by now? Had a reprieve already come? Or did St Peter himself refuse to sound the death knell of this poor young man? His eyes blindfolded, his hands losing their feeling with the tightness of the ropes, Neville could not judge what time had passed. Still he strained his ears for the sound of the bell. But half an hour went by, and it did not ring.

Then, with a noisy commotion which startled everyone, a rider galloped into the square.

'Reprieve! Hold off! Reprieve! A

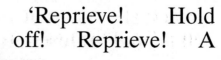

reprieve from the King!'

At the foot of the ladder, the crowd swept Neville Audeley along with them in a mad stampede for the church. The streets were dark: it was way past curfew, and yet curfew had not rung! Now they were free to satisfy their curiosity as to why.

As they got there, the bellringer had just finished climbing the long succession of ladders to the top of the belltower. He peered ahead of him in the shadowy belfry, mobbed by bats. At first he mistook the pale figure for a ghost. Then he saw it for what it was.

Nell had climbed up the tower and, despite the dizzying drop below her, leapt out to clasp the bell's huge clapper, wrapping her arms and legs around it like a lover, cloaking and muffling it with her clothing and hair. A hundred times and more the bell rope had swung her against the great brass wall of the bell, and yet she had not let go. Sickened by the motion, battered and bruised by the crushing impact, she had still refused to let the bell sound, refused to lose her grip, refused to die.

Half insensible, she refused even now to let go until the people called up to her through the wooden platforms of the tower: 'He's safe! Your sweetheart is safe!' Only then did she allow her hands to be prised from its clapper, and permit the bellringer to carry her down the tower across his shoulder. '. . . must not ring . . .' she repeated, over and over, without opening her eyes, '. . . must not ring tonight . . .' until, at the church door, Neville's kisses finally silenced her.

Originating in Chertsey, Surrey, this story was so popular that it spread far and wide, balladeers taking liberties with the details. It even crossed the Atlantic to America where the song, still sung today, came into being:

Hang on the bell, Nelly
Hang on the bell!
Your poor daddy's locked in a cold
*   prison cell.*
As you swing to the left and you
*   swing to the right,*
Remember the curfew must never
*   ring tonight!*

THE PRINCES IN THE TOWER

1483

'Mother, Mother, who are the boys in the velvet coats who came to the Tower today with all those servants and fine baggage?'

'That is Prince Edward, my dear— king as shall be—and his brother Richard. Their father is newly dead of a fever, and soon Edward will be crowned. Think of that!'

'Poor souls,' said Mary.

'Why do you say that? The Tower of London isn't all dungeons and guardrooms, you know. The state apartments are very fine.'

'No, no. Poor boys to have lost their father, I mean,' said Mary.

*   *   *

'Mother, mother, *when* is Prince Edward going to be crowned? I see him and his brother playing in the gardens and on the battlements, but the coronation never comes . . . They look sadder than they did. Only today I heard a servant call out: "My Lord Bastard!"'

'Ah, child. There'll be no coronation now. It is held that Edward was born illegitimate. He cannot be king. Their uncle is crowned instead: King Richard III.'

'Poor boys,' said Mary.

'Mmm, but to be king at twelve, and to carry the whole weight of government on those narrow shoulders. It would have been a hard life for the boy.'

'No, not to lose the crown, I mean,' said Mary. 'Poor boys, to be called such names by their own servants.'

*   *   *

'Mother, Mother, why do the princes never play in the Tower gardens any more? I see them at the windows, looking out, and they look so sad and pale.'

'I think, child, that their palace has

become a prison, and they are kept locked up tight, for fear some politicking nobleman argues that Edward is true King. So many factions. So many ambitious men. The world is a wicked place these days, my dear.'

'Poor souls,' said Mary.

'To be squabbled over like a hand of cards? Yes, my dear.'

'No, no. Not to be able to play out-of-doors, I mean,' said Mary.

*   *   *

'Mother, Mother, where are the princes? I never see their faces at the window any more.'

'Sshsh, my dear. No more questions. Best to keep silent in these wicked times.'

'Tell me. I want to know. What has become of the princes?'

'Very well. I shall tell you what is said. They say that the King—King Richard, that is—gave the orders. He chose the most ambitious man at court, and told him, "Do it." James Tyrrell was eager to "oblige" the King in

49

anything. So he summoned two men, his keeper of horse, John Dighton and Miles Forest who looks after—looked after—the princes.

'The boys were asleep together in the one bed, their arms tight round each other. Forest took hold of a feather pillow, Dighton another . . .'

'Oh Mother, no!'

'. . . and they pressed the pillows over the boys' faces. The sleepers woke, of course, and struggled, but what could two little boys do against two grown men? After a while they stopped struggling. Forest and Dighton hid the bodies, and it was as if those little princes had never lived.'

'King Richard did that? But why?' asked Mary. 'He already had the crown! Why did he need to kill them?'

'Hush, child, speak lower. If he did order it done, then it did him no good. Richard himself is dead—killed in battle—and there's a new king crowned. A Tudor king. King Henry VII. He says that Richard killed the princes in the Tower. So keep quiet, little child, and say no more. These are not times to question what we are told.'

'Poor souls,' said Mary.

'Yes. They were only children. No older than you, after all.'

'I did not mean the princes, Mother. I meant us. To live like pawns in a chess game and never know enough to tell black from white.'

The Wars of the Roses (1455–87) was a time of turmoil, with factions forming alliances, then betraying each other. The crown kept changing hands. That is why it is so difficult to arrive at the truth of what happened to the princes in the Tower.

Some 200 years after their disappearance a box was unearthed by builders. It contained the skeletons of two children aged about ten and twelve—probably, but not certainly, the princes. The bones were interred in Westminster Abbey.

After defeating Richard III at the battle of Bosworth, Henry Tudor set about systematically blackening Richard's name. All at once Richard was a hunchback, a child killer, a psychopath. (Shakespeare, living under a Tudor monarch, helped greatly in this reshaping of history, casting Richard as the arch villain.) Historians think Henry (whose own claim to the throne was not strong) might equally have ordered the killings. So might Henry Stafford, Duke of Buckingham, who may have been waiting his chance to usurp both Henry and Richard.

A RECIPE FOR SIMNEL CAKE

1487

Take one country, nervous and unsettled.

Take one king, newly crowned and with a shaky claim to the throne.

Add ambition. Take a gamble.

Take one fifteen-year-old: Lambert Simnel.

Spread thickly the rumour that *he* is the rightful heir to the throne.

Whip up the Irish and a few English lords.

Raise an army.

*   *   *

Lambert Simnel was pretending to be the Earl of Warwick.

The priest called Father Symonds had tutored Lambert well. By the time he turned up in Ireland, he carried himself like an earl, could speak intelligently about affairs of state, and seemed to be acquainted with all the lords and ministers of court. He was handsome and pleasant, and people instantly warmed to him. They listened with bated breath to the thrilling account of his escape from the Tower of London, where wicked King Henry VII had locked him up.

The Irish sank to their knees and paid homage. They also swore to put this wronged boy back in his rightful place: the throne of England.

In fact, Father Symonds was banking on the fact that the Earl of Warwick had been murdered by King Henry. Secretly. Unwitnessed. What could the King say, then, when this 'escaped Earl of Warwick' suddenly announced to claim his rightful crown? 'You are an impostor; I have already murdered the real Earl of Warwick'? Hardly.

And Father Symonds' obedient, talented protégé had managed to convince the Irish. Lambert Simnel knelt at the altar rail of St Patrick's Cathedral, Dublin. The crown was placed on his shining blond hair, and a fanfare acclaimed him Edward VI, *rightful* King of England.

There were only two drawbacks Father Symonds had not foreseen. In point of fact, Henry VII had *not* murdered Edward, Earl of Warwick: he was still alive! Secondly, Edward, Earl of Warwick, was *not* a handsome, intelligent, well-informed young man. He was a gormless ninny, as everyone knew who had ever met him.

King Henry fetched out the real earl, and paraded him through the streets of London, saying, 'Speak to him! Anyone may speak with him! Ask him who he is!' It seemed a simple way to prove that the rumours from Ireland were all nonsense.

'Ah, well yes, he *would* produce an

impostor,' argued Father Symonds, 'and pass him off as the real earl. But we know the real one, do we not? We have met the true Edward Plantagenet!'

Some believed him in all sincerity. Some simply *chose* to believe him since, to them, any usurper was preferable to the upstart Henry VII.

Francis the First Viscount Lovell, for instance, was ready to throw in his lot with the young 'King Edward VI'. So, too, was the Earl of Lincoln.

But Lincoln had met the real Edward Plantagenet many times in the past. So what expression crossed Lincoln's face when he met the boy impersonating him? Surprise? Amusement? Whatever thoughts went through his mind, he bent and kissed the hand of Lambert Simnel, and his face betrayed not a qualm, not a doubt.

Perhaps Father Symonds miscalculated. Perhaps, by the time he found out the Earl of Warwick was still alive, he was in too deep to turn back. Perhaps he staked too much on the unpopularity of Henry VII. The English lords who rose up in support of

'King Edward VI' brought with them a few household armies; the Irish brought daggers and short swords. Altogether, they were no match for the army which came against them at Stoke. King Henry fought his rival for the throne, and won.

Lincoln was killed and Lovell fled, their hopes and fortunes dashed. Lovell made for his house at Minster Lovell, and hid in an underground room. 'Lock the door and make it secret,' he told a servant. 'I have not been here, you understand? You have not seen me—or the King will have my head before the week's out!'

Father Symonds and Lambert Simnel did not slip so easily through the King's fingers. They were caught at once, and people winced to think what hideous punishment awaited them.

To everyone's astonishment, Henry VII, far from loosing the full might of royal justice on his enemies, seemed mildly amused by the whole affair. He invited the rebel lords to dine with him, and as they sat there, a serving boy came to serve them each with meat.

They looked once, they looked twice. An earl choked on his bread and grabbed for a cup of wine. It was! It had to be! The last time they had seen this boy, they had bent their knees and bowed their heads and sworn everlasting fealty to him and his descendants. It was Lambert Simnel. Henry had cut off neither his head nor his hands. 'I have put him to work in the scullery,' said Henry brightly. 'He turned the spit where your meat was cooked tonight, so if it is underdone, you can blame—well, you may blame the King, I suppose!'

Lambert Simnel must have given satisfaction in the King's kitchen, for within a few years he had risen to the post of royal falconer.

There is a tradition that Lambert, while working in the King's kitchen, invented the Simnel cake one Eastertime. A spicy fruit cake, flavoured with almonds, he topped it with eleven marzipan balls, in token of the eleven faithful disciples. The twelfth was missed off, of course, because

Judas, the twelfth disciple, betrayed Jesus. And nobody likes a traitor.

The Lambert Simnel episode is most remarkable for the way Henry VII handled it. Instead of applying the tyrannical cruelty of earlier ages, he used a lightness of touch which amazed and amused everyone. Afterwards, he was called 'the Solomon of English kings'.

In 1708, during building work at Minster Lovell mansion, a locked subterranean room came to light. Inside, the skeleton of a man sat with his head resting on a table, as if asleep. As the door opened, both clothes and bones crumbled to dust. Could this have been Francis, First Viscount Lovell? Did his servant run away, fearing arrest? Or was he simply too stupid to realize that a young man entombed below his own house needs food and water to survive?

THE FAERY FLAG

1490

The wife of the fourth laird of the MacLeods led him by the hand to a bridge near Dunvegan, and kissed him on the cheek. 'Twenty years I have been a wife to you, MacLeod,' she said, 'and twenty years I have kept secret my birth and parentage.'

'What do I care where you come from or who your parents were?' he said bluffly. 'You've been a good wife to me. Better than most.'

'That's because I am different from most. I am a fairy,' she said, 'and being a fairy, I came only for a while. I must go back now to my land. But before I do, I have a present to give you, in token of the love that has been between us.' And she gave him Britach Sith: 'the Faery Flag'. 'If ever the clan of the MacLeods is in mortal danger, unfurl this banner, and the tide of fortune will turn. Three times its magic will come to your family's aid.' Then she stepped away from him, over the parapet of the bridge, and disappeared like the spray of the water beneath.

Now the bold MacLeods are not people to ask help of anyone, especially the fairies. And though the fourth laird treasured the banner, at Castle Dunvegan—a memento of his faery wife—he never unfurled it. Nor did his children.

But a hundred years later, when a future laird was born, a slight, diaphanous figure was glimpsed within the castle walls one day, descending the stairs from the room which held Britach Sith. The baby's nurse saw the wraith cross to the cradle and (though she feared the child would be stolen away to the Land of Faery or replaced with a changeling) she could neither move nor cry out. Singing a strange, lamenting tune, the fairy tenderly wrapped the baby in the flag and began to rock him in her arms. Then she laid him back in the cradle.

After she had gone, her tune stayed lodged in the nurse's brain like a

splinter in a finger. Singing it, she found she had the power to soothe the loudest crying. Never again was a nurse employed to care for any heir to the MacLeod estates unless she had learned the faery lullaby from her predecessor. And yet still no human hand had unfurled the banner for its real purpose—to summon aid. The

MacLeods were Scotsmen, and Scotland is a land of granite.

In battle, the Faery Flag was guarded by twelve of the finest men, each one holding a rope tied to the flagstaff, so that Britach Sith might never fall to the enemy. But what enemy could stand, anyway, in the face of the ferocious MacLeods, beards piled on their chest, red hair flying?

None but the MacDonalds.

At Glendale, MacDonalds as numberless as the thistles on the braes, came clamouring down to the noise of drum and fife, and hemmed in the MacLeods.

'The Faery Flag! Unfurl the Faery Flag!' came the cry, and the Twelve Finest unfurled the banner from its pole-head with a century of creases kinking its silken design.

Perhaps the sun came out to shine in the MacDonalds' eyes. Perhaps magic threads entwined themselves in the hearts of the MacLeods. Either way, before sunset, the glen was strewn with dead MacDonalds, and the day belonged to the MacLeods.

Back and back came the MacDonalds intent on revenge, numberless as the tics on the heather. At the battle of Waternish, thirty years later, the MacLeods of Clanranald once more faced destruction at the hands of their age-old enemy.

'The Faery Flag! Britach Sith or we die!' came the cry, and the little silken bundle at the head of the flagstaff licked out like a dragon's tongue over the heads of the Twelve Finest.

Suddenly, the MacDonalds' charge faltered and stumbled to a halt, the men behind cannoning into those leading. Claymores dropped from hands weak with fright, and the hardest men of the glens turned tail and fled. For marching down on them they saw an army of 10,000 men, bright with raised weapons, russet with jutting beards and wild red hair. Whether the light had tricked them or whether magic fibres of the flag had strangled their courage, the battle was a rout, and victory went to the MacLeods.

Many wars have washed over the purple hills of Scotland and stained the glens with blood. And many more MacLeods have travelled to dangers farther afield. But the Faery Flag has yet to be unfurled a third time. It lies folded within Castle Dunvegan, awaiting the third and last cry of 'The Faery Flag! The Faery Flag! Unfurl the Faery Flag!'

Some believe the Faery Flag to have come to Scotland with the Norwegian king, Harald Hardraade, when he set out to conquer England in 1066. He flew a flag which he called Land-Ravager, a magic flag which, once unfurled, supposedly brought destruction to any enemy. On his journey south to fight King Harold, he lost Land-Ravager somewhere among the lochs and glens of Scotland.

Even in this century, during the First and Second World Wars and on battlefields far away from the braes,

men of the MacLeod clan carried photographs of Britach Sith over their hearts. Some of them even came home again, their photographs as creased and tattered as the flag itself.

TYNDALE'S CRIME

1536

Let me tell you about Tyndale. Who am I? Nobody much. In fact, I won't tell you my name, or I'll be in trouble with the authorities again. But to my mind, William Tyndale was one of the great men of all time. And now they've burned him. Like a log of wood, they've burned him.

He studied at Oxford and Cambridge; he was a brilliant scholar—could speak five languages! His colleagues had nothing but good to say about the man. But when he set about translating the New Testament from Latin into English, for the common people to read, suddenly he was a criminal. He had to go abroad to get it done.

'If God spares my life, ere many years I will cause the ploughboy to know more of the Scriptures than you do,' he told his learned colleagues

before he went.

Even abroad they hounded him. Some villain overheard the printers talking about the new book they were working on: Tyndale's New Testament. 'What a revolution this will stir up in England!' the printers said, and this eavesdropper thought, Revolution? Here's news the authorities will want to know about.

When they raided the printers, only the first ten sheets had been run off. But William was too quick for them. He had those ten sheets rolled up in his pack, and he was away to another city before they could lay hands on him.

He was in danger the whole time, every day of every year, but he pressed on with his work. Two editions were printed finally—one large, for reading aloud in public, one small enough to fit in a man's pocket. Anyone's pocket. Yours and mine.

He needed help, naturally, to distribute them. An association of European merchants, regularly travelling to and fro across the Channel in the course of their business, hid Tyndale's little printed Bibles among their goods. The books sold for two shillings, in shady corners and at back doors—black-market Bibles, selling like smuggled rum. There were 6,000 in the country before the bishops even knew what was happening. Everyone wanted one. *I* wanted one. I don't ever remember wanting a thing so much, or prizing anything so dearly as that parcel slipped into my hand one rainy day on Sheep Street.

All the clever men, the scholars and bishops bleated that it was an 'ignorant piece of work', riddled with errors. What did a few errors matter to the likes of us who had always been shut out from understanding, because nobody taught us Latin? We knew it was an excuse. We knew they wanted to keep God to themselves—not share Him about. 'Pearls trampled under the feet of swine,' was how they put it. We didn't care. We had the Word of God in our own hands at last, in our own language. My old mother learned to read, specially to be able to read Tyndale's Bible.

When they couldn't track down the printing presses, they bought up thousands of finished copies and burned them in great bonfires. But the more they burned, the more people wanted to know what it was they were missing.

So the King made it illegal to own a Tyndale Bible.

Troopers searched high and low, in

bread ovens and mangers and haylofts. Anyone found owning a Bible or reading one was put in prison for a month. I was one.

It was Shrove Tuesday, 1527. There were six of us. They dressed us up in penitential robes and gave us candles to carry, and faggots of wood. And there was this great parade through the streets—a public humiliation. We had to kneel on the ground and beg forgiveness from the people for our 'crime'. Then we were led three times round a bonfire—had to fuel it with those faggots of wood—and they made us throw our Bibles into the flames.

It was like throwing my very heart, I can tell you. It's hard to put into words, but I hated myself for doing it. Tyndale had given us this great book and here I was, destroying his years of work, *apologizing* for the joy he had given me. Of course I never meant a word of what I said that day. But I said it, even so. Like the apostle Peter denying Christ three times, to save his skin.

And now they've thrown Tyndale himself into the flames. Do you want to know his last words, before they strangled him at the stake and set him alight? 'Oh Lord, open thou the King of England's eyes.' That's what he said.

Well, you can burn a man and you can burn his books. But the truth won't burn, no more than water or milk. Fifty thousand copies of Tyndale's Bible have come into this country since the presses started up in Belgium. They might as well try to gather up the stars as to keep all those out of the hands of the people. It can't be done. Look here, hidden behind this panel in the wall: here's proof. Hold it. Open it. Read it. They will never stop up God's mouth—not now He's able to speak to us face to face, in Tyndale's English.

Tyndale's translations were not the first. As far back as John Wycliffe in the reign of Richard II, the Bible had been available in English. But copies of that had been hand-written and cost the great sum of £30 apiece, so they were scarcely meant for ordinary people.

Though Tyndale's translations were suppressed (of the first 15,000 volumes imported to England only three or four are left in existence) King Henry VIII was forced to acknowledge a need for a Bible in English. He therefore authorized a new translation—and the Great Bible came into existence.

These beautiful, large-format volumes were chained to church pulpits and read out at weekly services. People flocked to hear them in such vast numbers that the nobility and clergy must have taken fright. Within a couple of years Henry passed a law forbidding anyone to own or read or listen to readings from an English-language Bible unless they were of noble birth or a member of the clergy. Ordinary people were once again shut out. Two more reigns came and went before they were allowed access to the Word of God.

THE GHOST OF ANNE BOLEYN

1536

When the old queen died, Anne Boleyn and her train of ladies wore yellow dresses, in celebration. 'Now am I a queen indeed!' she said gleefully.

She had already won the heart of King Henry VIII away from his wife of eighteen years; in order to marry Anne, he had divorced Catherine. But now everyone would regard Anne as the true queen—even those who had questioned Henry's right to set aside his first wife. All that remained was for Anne to give Henry a child—a male heir—and their happiness would be complete.

She gave him a daughter— Elizabeth—but then Catherine had achieved *that* much. No, no. What Henry really wanted was a son, and Anne would give him that, too. Already she was pregnant again.

Turning the handle of the door,

Anne entered, already shuffling the handful of pretty phrases which she would deal the King if she found him there. Henry was there, but to her surprise, not alone. One of the ladies-in-waiting was sitting on his knee, giggling at some witty remark of his, her fingers sunk lovingly in his beard.

At the sight of Anne, Jane Seymour flinched; her cheeks flushed red. But Henry's big, fat-chopped face looked oddly calm, oddly undisturbed. He made no hasty move to slide the wench off his lap. 'Be at peace, sweetheart,' he said to Anne, 'and all shall go well with thee.'

Anne Boleyn stirred herself from frozen astonishment to shrill hysterics. One hand went to her round belly, the other to her forehead. She was hot. She

was cold. Tears pricked behind her eyes. She felt sick. The roaring in her ears told her she was about to faint.

The shock of finding her husband with another lady sent Anne into labour much too soon. The baby she was expecting—a boy—was born dead. Afterwards, Henry shouted at her for allowing 'the loss of his boy'. Anne reproached him for being the cause. But Anne had seen him wear that expression before—when people had counselled him against divorce, when people had spoken up for the ex-queen. Henry might just as well have shut the visor of a helmet: his face was all steel.

*   *   *

His love for Anne went out like a snuffed candle. All the fun had been in the chase and the wooing. Now he had seen another pretty face and he wanted to have it. Anne Boleyn was headstrong and gave herself airs. Saucy little Jane Seymour was far more agreeable, far more accommodating. No one had been able to stop him changing wives before—indeed his toadying ministers had smoothed the way to it. And if he could do it once, what was to stop him doing it again? The toadies would arrange it.

So he cut Anne Boleyn adrift.

There are always a ready supply of people who will say anything for money, or because they have been told to. A good lawyer can whip up a whisper of gossip—the smallest, spiteful rumour—into a mountain of damning evidence. Before long Anne was accused of being unfaithful to Henry with a whole host of men—even her brother. Accusations were flung like clods of mud, until the truth disappeared altogether. Henry had no interest in the truth—only the outcome. The Queen must die, so that he could marry Jane Seymour.

He un-married Anne. He un-queened Anne. He sent for a swordsman to cut off her head.

Getting up at two in the morning, she said prayers till dawn. Later, she sent for Sir William Kingston and said, 'I hear I shall not die afore noon, and I am very sorry therefore, for I thought to be dead by this time and past my pain.'

'The pain will be little,' he said, his eyes fixed awkwardly on the carpet at her feet.

Anne nodded. 'I have heard say the executioner is very good,' she said, putting both hands round her throat, 'and I have a little neck.'

In the morning of 19 May 1536, Henry VIII went hunting in Richmond Park. He was restless and excitable as he stood beneath the shade of a large oak tree and the eager hounds turned and leapt and yelped on their leashes. Across the park came a dull roar—the signal gun being fired at the Tower of London.

'Aha! The deed is done!' cried Henry jubilantly punching the air with both fists. 'Uncouple the hounds and away!' Next day, when he became betrothed to Jane Seymour, he wore a white silk suit—a sort of fancy-dress intended for gala days.

*   *   *

But Anne Boleyn's spirit was not so easily done down. Her headless ghost leads a nightly procession of phantom knights and ladies through the Tower, down to the chapel of St Peter-ad-Vincula within the Tower's precinct, where her body was interred. And every 19 May, a ghostly coach drawn by four headless black horses drives up to the gates of Blickling Hall where Anne was born. In it sits a ghost, her severed head resting in her lap. Meanwhile her father's accursed spirit is chased by a pack of shrieking demons over forty Norfolk bridges from midnight till dawn: an everlasting penance for giving his daughter into the hands of a murderer.

ANNE BOLEYN

Never before had a woman's blood been spilt on an English scaffold. It was an unprecedented wickedness. When Jane Seymour died, after giving birth to a son, Henry married Anne of Cleves for political reasons, but had the marriage annulled (see page 99).

He beheaded his fifth wife, Catherine Howard, on much the same charges as Anne Boleyn. His sixth wife, Catherine Parr, outlived him, her wifely duties reduced to tending a gross, diseased old man through his protracted final days.

Anne Boleyn's ghost appears in more places than any other. No fewer than five country houses attest to hauntings, not to mention the Tower. It was of her ghost that the song was written which runs:

> *With her head tucked*
> *   underneath her arm*
> *She walks the Bloody Tower*
> *With her head tucked*
> *   underneath her arm*
> *At the midnight hour . . .*

'LITTLE JACK HORNER
SAT IN A CORNER'

about 1537

Little Jack Horner sat in the corner of
the inn, the Christmas pie on the table
in front of him. He was deeply
depressed. What would become of the
animals, he wondered; of the fish in the
ponds, of the crops in the fields, of the
books on the shelves, of the wines in
the cellar? What would become of the
tenants who rented their land from the
monasteries, of the church plate and
the saintly relics? And what would
become of him, if the abbey ceased to
exist?

He knew the answer to all but the
last. Everything would go to the King—
that insatiable, Godless villain, Henry
VIII, who had set about disbanding
holy communities a thousand years old.
Perhaps during Jack's service the odd
teaspoon or bottle had found its way
into his pocket, but on the whole he

considered himself an honest, loyal, hard-working servant. But where would loyalty and hard work get him if the monastery were dissolved? He would lose his position, his livelihood, his home. Would his master still employ him when that master became plain 'Richard Whiting, Gent', rather than Abbot of Glastonbury?

Horner eyed the pie. Well, perhaps the bribe would work after all, and Glastonbury would be spared. Jack did not hold out much hope. He had heard what happened to other monasteries—their treasures confiscated, their statues smashed, their monks turned out of doors. Jack failed to see how one Christmas pie was going to persuade the King of England to spare Glastonbury. Even this one.

Jack had helped to 'bake' it. He had fetched the deeds from the abbot's great oak chest, rolled them tight and bent them round until all twelve fitted inside the pie dish. Then he had watched as the baked pastry lid went on. It was like the old nursery rhyme: 'four-and-twenty blackbirds baked in a pie' . . . Only this pie had twelve surprises inside it: the deeds to twelve manorial estates owned by Glastonbury Abbey. The bribe was supposed to persuade King Henry not to close down the abbey.

'That's a fair pie you have there,' the inn-keeper said, startling Jack Horner who was lost in thought. 'You'll not be wanting supper, then?'

'Yes, yes!' said Horner. 'The pie's not mine. It is a present for the King. Bring me something hot, please, and a mug of porter.'

After the first, Jack drank several more mugs, and the more he drank, the deeper he sank into brooding melancholy. What did the King of England want with twelve Somerset estates? What had he ever done to deserve them? Loyalty and hard work ought to count for something! Jack Horner clumped an angry fist down on the table. The pie jumped. Its pastry lid came loose.

The fingers of Jack's other hand went up to his mouth. What had he done? One corner of a deed showed white like a piece of tripe. Little Jack Horner glanced around the dimly lit inn. No one was looking. The document slipped out of the pie easy as winking. The pastry slipped back into place. Then, with trembling fingers, Jack broke the wax seal, pulled the ribbon . . .

Mells in Somerset.

It was the best estate of all the twelve. The plum. Horner knew its spreading beech trees, its stew ponds and hayricks, its skylines and rambling manor house. He closed both hands around the document and kissed it.

Well? Weren't eleven manors bribe enough for anyone? King Henry would never know there had been twelve to start off with. If the abbey were dissolved, then better that Mells should be kept back. If Henry spared it—well, then, Jack would always return the deed to Abbot Whiting, and be thanked for saving it.

A log settled in the grate and Jack guiltily crammed the parchment under his jacket. It lay over his heart, muffling the quick beat. He tried to summon the landlord, but the voice cracked in his throat. He breathed deep and tried again. 'Landlord! A drink for everyone here, and have one yourself!'

Drinkers looked around, smiling. Horner felt a glow of pleasure.

'Thank you kindly, sir, and who shall I tell folks is treating them?'

'Tell them: "a man of property". Tell

them: "the Master of Mells", my good man. Jack Horner of Mells in the county of Somerset.'

This story is reputedly the origin of the nursery rhyme, 'Little Jack Horner sat in a corner, eating his Christmas pie.' Jack Horner was indeed steward to the abbot of Glastonbury during the reign of Henry VIII. Presumably the bribe of the Christmas pie failed: Glastonbury was dissolved.

Corruption was rife in monastic communities of sixteenth-century England. Whereas some monks and nuns kept their vows, others led luxurious, immoral lives, outside reach of the law. But what began as a necessary 'cleaning up' of the monasteries quickly got out of hand.

Since the crown seized the proceeds, Henry VIII gained a fortune from each closure. He got greedy. Soon his commissioners were using any excuse to shut down monasteries, colleges, hospitals. The King's officers then went in, stripped out all valuables and took them to London. Locals rushed to take what was left: masonry, doors, windows—anything portable. Beautiful buildings were reduced to ruins. It has been called the Great Pillage.

THE FLANDERS MARE

1540

Henry rested his hands on his belly, and contemplated the two paintings. What a masterly painter Holbein was! And what a statesman Cromwell had been to track down two such handsome girls! Lutherans, too! A marriage to one of these princesses would endear him to half Europe, as well as filling that cold space in his life left by the death of his third wife.

Poor little Jane. He mourned her even now—even though he detested wearing black. At the cost of her own life, she had given him a boy child, a male heir, and for that he would always thank her. But a man cannot be expected to do without a wife; not a man of such royal appetites as Henry VIII. One more glance at the portraits, and Henry made his choice: the older girl, Anne. What though she could play no music? There are more important attributes in a wife.

Anne was wooed, and Anne was won, though not by Henry in person: he left all that to his diplomats. Anne was sent for and Anne came, crossing the Channel in the depths of winter. The closer she came, the more impatient he grew to see her. So, summoning seven gentlemen of about his own age, he told them to put on grey overcoats and saddle up: they were all riding to Rochester. Behind their obliging smiles, he glimpsed a certain unwillingness, given the filthy weather, but he just could not wait another moment to see his future bride! Henry, too, called for his horse to be saddled and for a grey overcoat to wear.

Eight anonymous gentlemen, all in grey, rode to Rochester, where Anne of Cleves had paused on her journey to London. What a surprise she would have, that beauty from Flanders, when her betrothed suddenly appeared and presented her with a New Year present of tippet and muff, and along with them his undying devotion!

The surprise was mutual.

What did the princess think, still queasy from the crossing, when she first saw her bridegroom? A mountain of bejewelled lard, sweating cheeks bulging through a square beard, eyes piggy with outrage. When she reverently fell to her knees before him, she could smell a whiff of disease from his lap and legs and feet.

What did Henry think when he first saw his bride? Nothing that could be put into words. He simply stared at that pock-marked face, that stocky body, that nose. The hands she thrust into his were dry as pigskin. When she spoke to him in some ugly, guttural language he did not understand, he could not get away quickly enough.

Thomas Cromwell would pay for this.

'Alas! Whom shall men trust? She looks like nothing so much as a great Flanders mare!' blared the King.

The official meeting of bride and groom at Blackheath scarcely went any better. Admittedly, inside a brocaded tent, with music and quantities of warmed wine within reach, Henry found it easier to be civil. But no one had the right to be as ugly as that! He felt duped. He had been sold a pup. Thomas Cromwell must get him out of this marriage or face the consequences.

The lawyers picked over the princess's life as if checking for nits. But though she had been betrothed as a child to someone else, the law said it was not enough of an impediment. Furthermore, the King's allies would be seriously offended if the wedding were called off. 'Is there then no other remedy but I must put my neck into the

yoke?' bayed the King.

Cromwell would pay with his: one neck for another. Even as Henry placed the wedding ring on Anne's finger, he was thinking how to be rid of her. She was, after all, his fourth wife, and a man who takes four wives can always take a fifth . . .

The wedding over, the bride was quickly dispatched to Richmond 'for the good of her health'. Her ugliness was a crime, pure and simple: a kind of treason. He owed it to his people to be rid of her. Besides, Henry had seen a face he much preferred.

Archbishop Cranmer, having just performed the marriage, dutifully listed all the reasons why it should be dissolved. Convocation declared it null and void. Parliament stifled its groans and passed a Bill to the same effect. All eyes turned on Cromwell, who had masterminded the

99

marriage: yet another over-ambitious man brought down by trying too hard to please: yet another casualty of the King-who-liked-marrying.

Meanwhile, Anne of Cleves was approached in private, by flattering, diplomatic men, and offered the chance to retire peacefully from her position as Queen and wife. They promised that her position at court would be that of the King's sister; no one would have precedence over her, except for the King's daughters and his future queen. And she should have £4,000 a year to live on.

Anne of Cleves sat in the window of Richmond Palace, one hand spread across her throat as she listened. She did not reply at once. Perhaps she was trying to choke back tears of disappointment. 'You may tell the King I live only to please His Majesty, and will act according to his wishes— though I hope I may be allowed sometimes to see the Princess Elizabeth who has become most dear to me.'

The French ambassador caught her

eye. The smile was so fleeting that he thought he must have imagined it, and yet so dazzlingly happy that, for a moment, the ex-Queen of England had appeared truly beautiful.

Six months later, the King was paying a visit to his ex-wife. The servants listening at the door heard laughter all afternoon. The Lady Anne had acquired a good grasp of the English language, and the King was as relaxed as anyone had ever seen him. Plainly, Henry and Anne were finding each other the best of company. She was witty and clever, well read and well bred. Best of all she was a good listener. While she sewed, the King talked, describing events at court, scandals uncovered, visitors up from the country, the word from overseas.

'Do you suppose they might be reunited?' whispered a lady-in-waiting sentimentally.

'He must lack company—a sick old man like that, surrounded by toadies.'

'Do you suppose he has come to claim her?' whispered an equerry.

But the King swept out again and

left, he in excellent good humour, she waving brightly from the window till he was out of sight. The Lady Anne seemed greatly cheered by the visit. Perhaps Henry had let slip that he was secretly married already to Catherine Howard.

Discussing remarriage, after Jane Seymour's death in childbirth, Henry asked Francis I of France to assemble a selection of pretty candidates for him to choose from. 'It is impossible to bring ladies of noble blood to market, as horses are trotted out at a fair,' retorted Francis. That is how Hans Holbein came to paint two pictures—of Anne and of her sister Amelia—so Henry could 'view' them without committing himself.

Unfortunately, Holbein omitted the smallpox scars which pitted Anne's face, and painted a flattering portrait. Cromwell's agents abroad, anxious to bring about the alliance, also reported nothing but good. Thomas Cromwell, when he saw the King's reaction, tried to duck the blame, but when he could not extricate Henry from the marriage, went to the Tower and was beheaded in July 1540. This is the man who had helped Henry become supreme head of the Church.

THE STAIRCASE

1560

The Queen, her head on one side, contemplated the portrait being held up by two equerries. The man in the picture was handsome—dashing, even. 'Hang it at the foot of my bed, where I can see it when I wake!' she said.

Elizabeth I was going through the motions—pretending to be contemplating marriage to yet another eligible suitor. This time it was an archduke—the man in the portrait. Before him there had been King Philip of Spain, the eldest Prince of Sweden, the Earl of Arran . . .

But those well acquainted with Elizabeth knew she cared nothing for any of them. She was not stirred by the archduke in the portrait, nor by any Spaniard, Swede or Scotsman. Elizabeth was in love with Robert Dudley, her master of the horse.

His relatively lowly station did not

matter (a commoner can soon be made a baron or an earl), nor did his father's execution for treason. No, there was only one small impediment to Elizabeth marrying her true love: Robert Dudley already had a wife.

'The Queen is only waiting for her to die,' wrote the Spanish ambassador in his letters home.

But why should Dudley's wife, Amy Robsart, die? A young woman in the prime of life? It was said by some that she was ill. Others said that she was all too healthy for Dudley's liking and that he was wondering how to change that.

*   *   *

Amy Robsart sat in the big dark house on Cumnor Hill. The servants had all gone out to the fair in nearby Oxford: she had insisted on them going, despite her pain and low spirits. Every night she rubbed the apothecary's lotion into her breast, but it seemed to do no good. Perhaps the pain came simply of a broken heart. For she was a woman whose husband did not love her—a woman who, just by continuing to breathe, blocked her husband's path to success and happiness. That was why she had not refused the wine at dinner, even though she feared it might be poisoned.

Not that Robert would do such a thing. Oh no, surely not her Robert who, in marrying her, had promised to cherish her. But the Queen—ah, the Queen's wishes could creep like ivy into every last crevice of her kingdom. Amy could feel those wishes entwining her, dragging on her, sapping her strength. A loyal subject ought to help the Queen to happiness, rather than hinder her.

The big dark house creaked and rustled around her, its corridors, landings and stairs unlit. It was not her own house. It belonged to a friend of Robert's. And Robert was away at court, as usual, dancing, paying compliments, exchanging witty remarks with the Virgin Queen. The pain in Amy's chest grew worse. The trees on Cumnor Hill put their heads together and whispered—gossip and rumour,

rumour and gossip.

*   *   *

Robert Dudley was out riding with the Queen when the messenger arrived from Cumnor. Terrible news, a tragic accident. 'What has happened?' asked Dudley.

'It's your wife, sir. Found yesterday, sir. A tragic fall, sir. The stairs . . .'

Amy Robsart lay spread-eagled at the foot of the staircase in the house at Cumnor Hill, her neck broken, her feet bare, her skin as pale as her nightdress. The coroner's jury brought in a verdict of accidental death. In the dark, unfamiliar house, she had tripped and fallen.

The other possibility—that she had committed suicide—could not be put into words, for that would have meant a suicide's burial in unconsecrated ground.

The public, however, were in no doubt as to what had happened. Dudley had wished his wife dead and now she was. In the public imagination, Robert Dudley was a murderer, and people hated him for it. The rumour-mongers whispered:

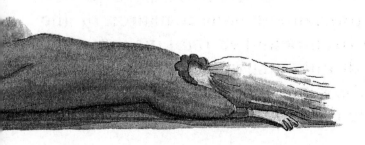

'Have you heard? The Queen is secretly married to Dudley!'

'She is making him Earl of Leicester.'

'She means him to rule England with her!'

'A murderer in the arms of our Queen!'

But they were all wrong. The truth was that Amy Robsart's suspicious death had made such a marriage impossible. Dudley was so unpopular now that Elizabeth would antagonize the whole country, her ministers and her allies by marrying him.

Concealed behind the red curls, the porcelain-white skin, the coquettish flirting, the bright, bird-like eyes, was a steely, calculating brain. If Elizabeth had ever considered marriage to the beautiful Robert Dudley, she shut her mind to it now. Love was sweet, but politics were crucial. Marriage to her, she proclaimed, 'was a matter of the weal [well-being] of the kingdom'. She would only marry if it were in the country's best interests.

She did indeed make Robert Dudley

Earl of Leicester, and as he knelt before her to receive the accolade, she tickled his neck playfully and giggled. The courtiers turned to one another with raised eyebrows and meaningful looks. But they were entirely wrong. The earldom was intended to make Robert Dudley a fit suitor for a queen, but not Queen Elizabeth. She had suggested he should woo the troublesome Mary Stuart, Queen of Scots.

Elizabeth was Queen first, woman afterwards. She did not marry the man in the portrait, nor the Duke of Anjou, nor Emperor Charles IX, nor the Duke of Alençon, nor the Earl of Essex, nor any of the other suitors who wooed her. She was in her mid-twenties and yet she had no illusions left. She was a queen, and whoever smiled or bowed or sent her gifts or poetry or portraits was thinking chiefly of her crown, not her beauty.

She was a kind of staircase ambitious men wanted to climb.

Elizabeth never married, although Parliament and the country urged her to, and she assured them she would. She liked to keep suitors dangling for as long as possible, for while a suit continued, she was in a very strong position to negotiate.

Did Amy Robsart kill herself? Was she murdered on her husband's orders? Or by Sir William Cecil, the Queen's Secretary, who frowned on the romance and knew the scandal would force Elizabeth to shun Dudley? Or did Amy just trip in the dark and fall, her

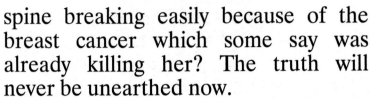

spine breaking easily because of the breast cancer which some say was already killing her? The truth will never be unearthed now.

Robert Dudley took a second wife in 1573 and married again, bigamously, in 1578. Elizabeth was fleetingly furious with him, but relented and, despite his poor military record, appointed him commander of forces against the Spanish Armada in 1588. That same year, however, he suddenly died: poisoned. Rumour had it that poison meant for his wife had somehow found its way into his own food.

WALTER RALEIGH SALUTES THE QUEEN

1580

It was no weather for finery. But Queen Elizabeth shone like the sun wherever she went (as she never tired of being told). So Walter Raleigh pulled on his finest shirt, with its wide, stiff ruff of pleated cotton at the throat. His manservant helped him into the stiff, bombasted brocade doublet and short-hose, then pulled the laces tight. (The bright lining showed through the slashed panels of the plump hose like segments of Seville orange.) He drew on his own pale, silvery, silk stockings and secured them with tasselled garter-ribbons above his knee. Then he slid his arms into the painted leather over-doublet and his feet into his new low-heeled, calfskin shoes which he fastened with ribbon bows. He buckled on his embossed swordbelt, then, last of all, swung round him his brand new cloak—a masterpiece of panned, piped, interlined, gilt-clasped, silver-corded velvet. Raleigh was about to meet the Queen of England for the very first time.

Magnificent as Raleigh looked, his outfit paled into shabbiness beside the Queen's finery. As she descended from her coach, the small boys who had chased three miles in its wake caught their breath and gasped. She was as marvellous as a galleon new-rigged, as an angel among shepherds. Her pale kid shoes might as well have belonged to a fairy-tale princess.

But this was not London. It was a country town. This was countryside overshadowed by forest, overhung with cloud, overrun with mud. Elizabeth hesitated and looked around her, with obvious unease, skirts bunched within her two fists, to lift them clear of the dirt. Across her path lay . . . a large, brown puddle.

A cold, spitting rain fell on Walter's hair as he took off his hat and bowed low. A cold, reproachful blast of wind ruffled his cuffs as he unfastened his splendid cloak. Then, with a bull-fighter's flourish (but the careless expression of one who does such things every day) Walter Raleigh laid down his cloak. He laid it down over the puddle—it made a soft, velvety squelch—inviting the Queen to walk over it rather than dirty her shoes.

The sight of that handsome velvet cloak lying in the mud made even Elizabeth catch her breath. She stared for a moment as the cloth grew sodden and settled, then she turned a dazzling smile at the owner. The glance lengthened as she took in his dashing good looks, his exquisite tailoring. Then she stepped on to the cloak, as carefully as a skater stepping on to the ice of a pond. Momentarily, the crowd glimpsed the pale prettiness of her shoe.

The cloak lay ruined, soaked. But as Walter said, with a shrug, to any who mentioned it, that was a small sacrifice to please a queen. Even the beaux and coxcombs strutting in the Queen's wake held handkerchiefs to their noses and whispered among themselves that it was 'cleverly done', even they admired the panache of it—the grand, chivalric flourish of it. Raleigh was a made man.

It is not known with any certainty whether the incident of the cloak actually took place—several towns lay claim to it—and whether it was this which first endeared Walter Raleigh to Queen Elizabeth I. Certainly he became a great favourite of hers after joining court at the age of thirty. She heaped gifts of land on him and sent

him on various missions of exploration
and conquest. But she never seems to
have found him reliable enough to
entrust with high office. He could not
intrigue as well as those around him
and eventually lost his head for
treason.

The cult of Elizabeth's beauty gave
rise to music, literature and art, even
after Elizabeth herself, vain to the last,
had decayed into a sad, painted old
lady with rotten teeth and a flame-
coloured wig. At the end, she sat up in
a chair for three days and nights for
fear, if she went to bed, death would
lay hands on her.

FRANCIS DRAKE AND
A GAME OF BOWLS

1580–1588

The sun rose bright and cheerful, but the bride did not. Lizzie Sydenham put on her wedding finery with a heavy heart. Her mother and father greeted her with little cries of admiration and happiness—'Fancy! Our little Lizzie a bride!'—but she could not smile.

Even so, she knew better than to say, 'I don't want to marry. I do not love this man.' So she took the nosegay of flowers from her mother and stepped out of doors for the short walk to church. What good would be served by defying her parents' wishes?

Her one true love was oceans away, attempting the impossible, trying to sail around the world. If he were not already dead, it would take several miracles to bring him safe home. Her parents said Francis Drake was a nobody, a rough, coarse, low-born pirate, for all the gold, silver and pearls he had stolen in the Spanish Main. Lizzie did not believe it, but when, after years of waiting, Francis still had not come home to claim her, what else could she do but accept the respectable, unremarkable gentleman waiting for her now at Stogumber Church? Suddenly, something made her look up.

It happened so fast: there was no dodging aside, no ducking down or turning to run. She stopped stock still, and with a massive thud which shook the ground and raised a spew of dust, a great round stone ball landed at her feet. It struck so hard that it half sank itself in the dirt. The little wedding party stared.

Lizzie's father said that it must be masonry from the church roof. Her mother said someone was trying to kill them. But Lizzie simply handed back her bouquet and said, 'I shan't marry today. Francis has fired a cannonball across the world to forbid it. He wants me to wait for him, so I shall.'

And she did. Nothing would

persuade her to break her vow. When Francis Drake sailed into Plymouth harbour, and all the church bells in the West Country welcomed him home, Lizzie Sydenham stood waiting.

The rock was not a cannonball at all, of course. Nothing so ordinary. It was a meteorite. While Drake's little vessel the *Golden Hind* sailed round the world, a fragment of debris from an exploding star had been voyaging through the vastness of space, to land at Elizabeth Sydenham's feet. The Spanish said Sir Francis Drake had a drum with which he could summon up the wind. They said he had a mirror in which he saw the future. They said that he had sold his soul to the Devil for mastery of the seven seas. But then the Spanish were superstitious, and their captains preferred not to admit that any Englishman could get the better of them. Ever since Drake had sailed up the River Tagus to Cadiz, and burned the King of Spain's warships, they had called him 'El Draco'—'The Dragon'— a beast of fire and destruction.

With Spain's fleet—its 'Invincible

Armada'—massing for war on the other side of the Channel, the English themselves liked to think that Drake possessed magic powers. They told how he had *made* the entire English fleet, sitting on a cliff one day, whittling a twig. Every splinter had turned by magic into a ship on the sea below.

The Spanish, on the other hand, had felled an entire forest, to build their fleet.

When the Armada finally attacked, the English admirals—Drake, Hawkins, Frobisher and Lord Howard of Effingham—were playing a game of bowls on Plymouth Hoe, a grassy flatness overlooking the sea. The pleasant knock of wood against wood was interspersed with talk of strategy, and jokes about Spanish beards.

Suddenly there was a shout, and a look-out came pelting along the Hoe: 'They're coming! They're coming! The Spanish fleet is sighted! They're coming!'

Snatching up gloves and sword belts, peering out to sea, the various commanders started for their ships at a

run. There were crews to turn out, gangplanks to raise, ropes to cast off, anchors to weigh, drums to be sounded, wives to kiss goodbye . . . The fate of the country was about to be decided.

'Hold hard, friends, hold hard!'

They turned back. Drake stood just as before, a cluster of bowls at his feet. 'Plenty of time to win the game and beat the Spaniards too!' he said, in

his slow, Devonshire drawl. And he bowled—slow and steady and true.

The other men walked back, laid aside their gloves, took their turns. Over the horizon a hundred topsails, like puffy white clouds, moved into sight. Crowds gathered along every quay and jetty and cliff, standing on tiptoe, craning their necks to see. But the English commanders finished their game before strolling sedately to their ships and giving battle-orders, for all the world as if they were ordering dinner.

*   *   *

The English ships were smaller, quicker and more manoeuvrable than the lumbering Spanish galleys and galleons. They could dart in close, loosing cannonfire and arrows. Drake used fire-ships, too—filled with kindling or gunpowder, helms lashed on collision course, while down below, the fuses burned . . . Fire ships wrought havoc among the Spanish fleet, blasting them out of the water or burning them down to their keels. El Draco could indeed breathe fire.

Even so, the Spanish sea captains believed that their honour depended on victory, and their honour was worth more to them than their lives. They fought with frenzied heroism, until blood ran in streams from their gunports and their ships foundered under them. Their commander-in-chief, the Duke of Medina Sidonia, was an incompetent, but they fought on despite him, till ammunition ran out on both sides, and the noise of battle fizzled into silence.

Then the Spanish beat north up the English Channel, planning to skirt the north coast of Scotland and sail home. That is the day, legend says, when Francis Drake went ashore, and danced with the witches and demons on a windswept clifftop, summoning up a storm.

Gales came in from the west. Damaged, leaking ships, manned by injured, hungry crews, wallowed lower and lower in the water. The storms, which raged for a fortnight, drove ships on to rocks, on to sandbars, into unfriendly harbours, or simply swamped them in deep water, leaving not a trace. Of 130 ships which set sail, just over half reached home, and of 27,000 men only some 9,000 survived to feel the Spanish sun on their faces. Then they lay in their mangled ships and died of fever, as though fate had damned every last man.

On his journey home overland, the

Duke of Medina Sidonia was pelted with stones by small boys for his disgraceful failure.

Drake went home to Lizzie. But ambition for gold and glory soon sent him back to plundering the Spanish Main. He died there, and was lowered to his eternal rest in the vaults of the sea.

DRAKE

The Spanish Armada of 1588 was doomed from the outset. Rotten provisions, leaks, storms, disease all conspired against King Philip's navy. The design of its ships was medieval and only suited to calm, clement seas. 'Drake's gales' were phenomenal—historic events in themselves. But none of this lessens the achievements of the English in defeating the Armada.

In Ireland, where many of the wrecks took place, you can still see faces with Mediterranean features which suggest that not all the shipwrecked Spaniards died. And even after 400 years, not all the missing ships have been accounted for.

By the time the crisis was over, fever was rife among the English sailors. When Queen Elizabeth heard this, she deliberately delayed paying them off until so many had died as to save her a third of the bill.

It is said that Drake's Drum, kept now at Buckland Abbey, can be used to summon Drake back if ever England is in peril.

Lizzie's meteorite is still at her family home in Somerset. He married her in 1585, but she was his second wife, no patient childhood sweetheart.

THE LONG-EXPECTED END

1587

Mary sprinkled sand over her letter, to stop the ink running, then shook off the surplus. It made a noise like voices whispering.

She had pondered long and hard whether to answer the letter from Anthony Babington. He was a dear, devoted, devout young man, but rash and passionate. He said he was planning to assassinate Queen Elizabeth and put Mary in her place.

So long as she did not actually *acknowledge* his suggestion, she could not be accused of conspiring with him. But surely a letter would be safe enough hidden inside the empty casks which left Chartley House?

Letters from her friends and supporters arrived in the full casks, and her own left in the empty ones. It was a fine, convenient arrangement and a great comfort to a woman kept under house arrest for the best part of twenty years. Mary folded the letter, and allowed her hand to rest on it, trembling. She had just given her consent to his assassination plot.

*   *   *

Mary Queen of Scots was Elizabeth's second cousin, a Catholic and a serious nuisance. She threatened the nation's stability. Every Catholic would have liked to see Elizabeth dead and Mary crowned in her place. Elizabeth, for her part, would have liked to see Mary dead and out of the way.

And yet they were cousins. Elizabeth must not seem unnaturally cruel to her own flesh and blood. It was a problem. Best if Mary should be discovered committing some gross act of treason, plotting some coup. So Elizabeth put her secret service to work, spying on Mary, keeping a watch on her and her friends, vetting all her visitors—intercepting all her mail.

So when Babington wrote to Mary of killing the Queen, and Mary wrote back, encouragingly, Sir Francis Walsingham, head of the Queen's secret service, read both letters. After all, it was he who had organized the business of the wine casks.

Mary was damned by that letter to Babington. Babington and his fellow conspirators were doomed men. Their plot gave Elizabeth just the excuse she had lacked all these years. Now she could put Mary to death.

In September, Babington and thirteen other conspirators were dragged through the streets of London on hurdles, face-up to the sky, to a scaffold of dizzying height where they were hanged, drawn and quartered.

Elizabeth's Council clamoured for Mary to be imprisoned at once in the Tower of London, but Elizabeth sent her to Fotheringay Castle instead—yet another secure house in the long line of comfortable prisons. At Fotheringay she was in the charge of Sir Amyas Paulet.

Tearfully Elizabeth received loyal deputations from her people calling for the death of the treacherous Mary.

With great shows of unwillingness, she finally allowed herself to be persuaded. Mary was guilty of treason. Wild delight met the announcement, with church bells ringing all day and bonfires lit in the streets. Elizabeth's adoring public bayed for Mary's blood. All Elizabeth had to do was agree.

Mary's son James pleaded for her life—but not very hard. He was in line to become King of England, and nothing must jeopardize that. He would be a fool, he wrote to a friend, 'if I should prefer my mother to the title'.

Elizabeth signed the death warrant . . . but would not give instructions for it to be sent. 'What a great relief it would be to me,' she murmured aloud, 'if some loyal subject were now to kill Mary . . .'

Amyas Paulet, Mary's prison warder, refused to take this heavy hint. He wrote back that he would not 'make shipwreck of his conscience without law or warrant'.

And so the warrant was sent—oh, quite against Elizabeth's will—an abuse of trust (she said), a wicked flouting of her will! She had never intended it to be sent! The man responsible would pay!

Even so, on Tuesday, 7 February, a hand knocked gently on the door of Mary's apartments and a gentleman informed her, with great civility and courtesy, that, 'Tomorrow morning, ma'am, you must die.'

Mary spent the night praying, then in the morning dressed entirely in black with a veil of white lawn over her auburn hair. At forty-four, her former beauty had faded. Years of enforced idleness, sitting over books or embroidery or letters had made her portly, with a fat face and double chin. Her shoulders stooped. And yet it was a dignified, fearless figure who was led into the great hall of Fotheringay Castle to be confronted by a scaffold draped in black, two executioners, a huge axe.

Her servants were beside themselves with grief, trembling, sobbing, swooning. Though Mary wept at being parted from them, her sole companions for so many years, she told them to be glad, not sorry. 'For now thou shalt see Mary Stuart's troubles receive their long-expected end.'

The executioners tugged inexpertly at her clothing. She smiled: 'I was not wont to have my clothes plucked off by such grooms.' Then she knelt at the block and prayed in Latin: 'Into your hands, O Lord . . .'

The axe fell; the room flinched with a single spasm at the noise of it. There

was a ghastly moment of unforeseen horror. The head was not off! The axe man took a second stroke.

He lifted the severed head up for all to see . . . and the auburn wig and the blood-stained white lawn came away in his hand, letting fall a head of close-cropped grey hair with two ringlets over the ears.

'God save the Queen!' said the headsman.

'Amen!'

'This be the end of all the enemies of Her Majesty!' said the Earl of Kent. But the communal cry of 'Amen' broke off, as the skirts of the dead woman began to stir.

Out at the hem nosed a little dog, whimpering and afraid. One of Mary's dogs. It trotted into the pool of blood between head and shoulders, and lay down, whining, inconsolable. Nothing could erase that image from the minds of those who saw it.

No more could Elizabeth's raging and protests and loud public regrets erase the impression that she had got her wish at last: Mary Queen of Scots was extinguished and Queen Elizabeth could sleep easy in her bed.

JAMES I

William Davison, Elizabeth's secretary (and innocent scapegoat) was accused of sending the death warrant to Fotheringay against Elizabeth's wishes. He was tried, fined and imprisoned in the Tower. No one seriously expected the sentence to be carried out, but Elizabeth insisted on it. Mary's

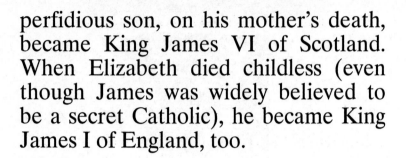

perfidious son, on his mother's death, became King James VI of Scotland. When Elizabeth died childless (even though James was widely believed to be a secret Catholic), he became King James I of England, too.

THE CITY OF RALEIGH

1587

The first English colonists to cross the Atlantic landed on Newfoundland, squabbled, fought, fell ill and gave up. Setting sail again for England, their ship went down with everyone aboard. So much for conquering the New World.

Roanoke Island, at first sight, seemed a far more promising place to begin. It rose out of the curved horizon, green and clad in trees. There were rumours of gold and pearls.

One hundred and seven settlers built a fort there. But instead of planting crops, they went hunting for gold. They quarrelled with the local people and ran desperately short of supplies. When a hurricane struck, they were so terrified that they begged a visiting ship to take them home. Sir Richard Grenville, calling at Roanoke, found no one there. He did his best to revive the settlement by landing fifteen men with enough provisions for two years.

In due course, Sir Walter Raleigh arrived with another group (this time including women and children). It was their task to found the 'City of Raleigh' in this land called 'Virginia' after the Virgin Queen Elizabeth. But where were Grenville's fifteen sailors? There was not a trace—except for one skeleton of a murdered man!

Undaunted, the settlers took over the deserted fort, built timber cabins, cleared land and planted it. A baby girl was born—she too was called Virginia. With just a few more supplies from England, the community would be able to survive the whole year round!

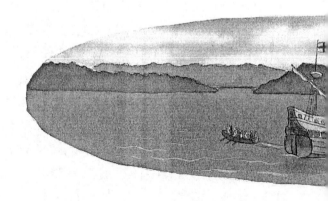

'I'll go myself and get them!' said John White, elected leader of the little community.

But when he reached home, he found that England had troubles of her own. War with Spain was brewing. The novelty of the New World had worn off, and nobody was interested in the troubles of a handful of settlers. It was two frustrating years before he could lead a relief expedition.

It was an anxious voyage for White. How many more children would have been born? Would tornadoes have struck? Or hostile natives? As the ship sighted land, the cheerful sight of rising smoke was a great relief to him.

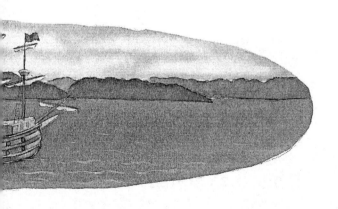

Then he realized that the smoke was a forest fire, nothing more. The ship fired its guns to attract attention. John White leaned eagerly over the rail, to see which of his friends would come running down to the beach: Mary, Ananias or even Virginia.

No one came.

It was getting late and there was a heavy sea running. Not until the next morning did the captain send two boats ashore. One overturned in the surf and seven people were drowned. But the survivors scrambled ashore. A trumpeter blew several blasts on his damp trumpet, and the rest broke raggedly into song.

*   *   *

There was no reply to their singing. Though they sang till their voices cracked, no one came. There was no one left to come.

Not a trace remained of the settlement. Not only had the people disappeared, but the cabins, too! Books lay around like dead birds, fluttered by the wind. But there was no Mary, no Ananias, no little Virginia Dare.

There were no graves, either, no skeletons or bloodstains. John White took heart from that. 'They have moved on. It was agreed among us: if a move was decided upon, they would leave word: a message carved on a tree—a cross beneath it if danger had driven them to it. Look for a sign. Look for a message!' And he ran from tree to tree, searching. 'Over here! Make haste, there's something here!'

There carved in a tree were just three letters: C R O. What did it mean? There was no cross underneath, but then perhaps the person who carved them had been prevented from finishing. Anyway, what sense could be made from three letters: C R O?

John White said, 'Croatoan. They have gone to Croatoan Island. The Croatoans are friendly. I am greatly joyed. It means my friends are safe!'

And with quite extraordinary confidence in those three crude letters, he set sail again for England. Incredibly, he did not make for

Croatoan Island or enquire any further. It was as if the people with whom he had been entrusted had simply gone on ahead of him to somewhere he could not follow.

The next time English ships happened to anchor off Croatoan Island, they found no trace of any English prisoners or settlers. Six expeditions Sir Walter Raleigh sent in search of the citizens of the City of Raleigh: they found nothing.

And yet 100 years later, Croatoans sided with the English in the War of Independence, saying that they had taken all their laws and religion from English settlers. Some had blue eyes, fair hair and beards. They told a legend at their firesides, too, of a little white maid who grew up into a beautiful woman, and then changed by magic one day into a white deer. Was that child Virginia Dare, born in hope, christened in thanksgiving, lost while the world was looking the other way?

When Captain John Smith landed at Jamestown in 1607, he heard tell that he was not the first: there were settlers already living inland. They had reputedly been taken there by Croatoan tribesmen. Some had been killed, some had escaped, including a little girl. It was also suggested that local agricultural processes and copper smelting had been learned from contact with white settlers.

Although the historical credit as 'founding fathers' usually goes to the

Pilgrim Fathers, they did not sail for the New World aboard the *Mayflower* until 1608, by which time the East Coast was quite well-trodden ground.

THE SPANISH GALLEON
OF TOBERMORY

1588

Not for the first time and not for the last, love came in a dream. Viola, the King of Spain's daughter, dreamed of a man, and his face was so fine and his whole bearing so kingly that she swore to find him, even if it meant sailing the world round. Past Scotland she came, to the island of Mull.

Her galleon, the *Florencia*, dropped anchor in Tobermory Bay, for the cliffs had the same ragged edges as in her dream. There indeed she found the man she had dreamed: MacLean of Duart. Viola thought her happiness would never end, that MacLean would marry her and make all her dreams come true. The man himself was hugely flattered. There was only one snag: MacLean of Duart already had a wife—a fiery Scottish wife who did not mean to lose her husband to the lady in the bay.

Wife MacLean took matters into her own hands, took a keg of gunpowder, too, and went aboard the *Florencia*. 'Leave my man be, ye black-eyed hussy!' she told Viola. 'Have ye not men enough in your country that you must come stealing ours?'

'I must go where my heart leads,' said Princess Viola. 'I was meant to marry MacLean: my dream told me so.'

Wife MacLean left the ship—left, too, her keg of gunpowder and a slow-burning fuse. Not all the Northern Lights on Midsummer Eve ever lit up the Hebridean skies like the explosion which rocked the galleon *Florencia* that day and scattered her to the four winds. The mast was shot like a harpoon at the whaley moon. Pieces of plank skimmed over the water. Only one soul escaped . . . the ship's cook, who was blown, by the force of the explosion, all the way from ship to shore.

Had the cook died in his galley, perhaps the fate of the *Florencia* might have remained a Hebridean secret.

150

Instead, word reached the King of Spain, who was filled with such spitting wrath that men fled him like a keg of gunpowder.

'Get you to Mull!' he told his trusted sea-captain. 'Kill the man MacLean, his wife and all his children! Kill his dogs and cats and the birds in his chimneys! Kill his servants and kinsmen and neighbours! Break down his walls and burn every blade of grass on Mull, for he has robbed me of my daughter, lovely as any dream!'

When MacLean of Duart saw the Spanish man o' war drop anchor in Tobermory Bay, his big stomach quaked and his heart beat so wildly that all thought of Princess Viola fell out of it. 'See what ye have done, ye foolish wife!' he whispered.

But his wife squared her square shoulders and stuck out her several chins. She summoned all of the eighteen witches of Mull, and pointed to the ship in the bay. Like frogs all hopping into the one pond, the eighteen witches of Mull pooled their eighteen magics, pooled their curses,

151

pooled their worst of wicked spells. Above the bay, they spread their arms, their feather-white shawls. Eighteen seagulls flew out to sea, circling and soaring, screaming fit to chill the blood of any fiery Spaniard.

The wind too began to scream, like a million gulls, and the waters of the bay swirled. The ship's mast turned like the

spoon in a mixing bowl. Then down went the ship, confusing sea foam with rich Spanish lace.

When the storm was spent, not a trace remained of the captain or his ship. Within a matter of years, only the ghost of a memory survived, faint as any dream.

A galleon *Florencia* probably did explode and sink in Tobermory Bay on the Hebridean island of Mull in 1588. It was one of the ships of the Spanish Armada sent by Philip of Spain to invade and conquer England. Defeated by Drake, scattered by storms, the fleet struggled to reach home by sailing round the coasts of Scotland and Ireland: many were lost on the way. The Scots and Irish, being Catholic, should have been sympathetic towards the bedraggled Spanish. But in those

days, shipwrecks were a ready source of booty, and shipwrecked mariners were not encouraged to survive.

News of the sea battle waged between England and Spain in the English Channel must have been very slow to reach the Hebrides. Even then it would have had precious little significance for the inhabitants of Mull. It is hardly surprising, then, that this local legend grew up to account for the galleon's visit in a more romantic way.

THE THEATRE THAT DISAPPEARED

1598

Richard Burbage tried every line of argument he knew. He began good humouredly, in comic vein: 'Where will the groundlings throw their apple cores if not at us actors?'

He pulled himself up to his full height (which was not great): 'Is this not the Age of Poesie? And are we not the finest of a fine profession, speaking verse of genius, holding up to humanity the bright likeness of its image?'

He tried again: 'My father built this theatre! It is the oldest and most visited in London—yeah, in the kingdom!'

He even tried darkest tragedy, and he was famous for his tragic roles. 'And wilt thou see us cast upon the mercy of the rude winds? Hoist up upon the shoulders of misfortune for want of a house over our untousled heads?'

But the landlord only crossed his arms, pursed his lips and scowled. 'I say the lease is up and that's an end. You actors can take your theatricals, Richard Burbage, and shift yourselves off my ground. The Theatre is closed, and there's an end!'

Burbage threw an arm across his eyes and struck the pose of a man betrayed by fate. But when he took his arm away, the landlord had gone. He was standing alone in the street. Tugging down his doublet, he replaced his hat at a rakish angle and squared his stocky shoulders. 'Very well, you wish the Theatre gone, do you? Then go it shall!' he said under his breath.

He went in search of his elder brother, Cuthbert, and told him to hire a cart. 'A big cart. Better still, five carts. Then find John and Francis and Will—everyone who's sober. We have work to do.' And as the light faded and the streets emptied, a caravan of carts negotiated the narrow lanes of London, southwards towards the river.

Lying in bed the next morning, the owner of the land, north of the city walls, where the Chamberlain's Company had acted night after night, mused on the value of the Theatre, now that its lease had expired. There was not much to be done with a circular building open to the elements in the centre. Cock fighting, perhaps, or a bear pit. Boxing, even. But all those were lewd and Godless pastimes and attracted lewd and Godless people . . .

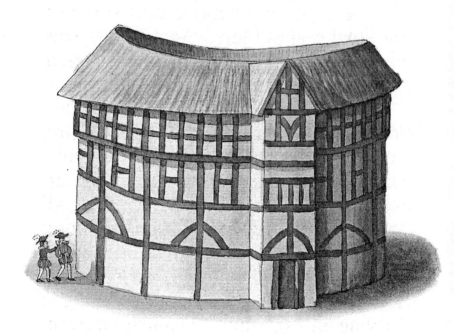

His wife threw open the window and emptied out the night-soil. She stayed there, pot upraised, her head outside, beyond the sill.

'Close the window, woman. I am in a draught. Did you hear that traffic last night? Horses and carts all night long.'

His wife drew her head back inside, but still stood holding the pot at shoulder height. 'It's gone,' she said.

'What's gone?'

'The Theatre. It has . . . walked in the night.'

'Fallen down, you mean?' He ran to the window, the noises of early-morning London rising up like starlings to circle his head. But there in a cityscape he knew as well as his wife's bumpy profile, was a hole. Where, the day before, the Theatre had stood lay a heap of thatching, a snow of plaster, and wattle enough to fence a field. All the timber uprights, and joists and beams and benches, all the barge boards and staging and duck boards and doors had gone, loaded aboard the Burbages' carts and trundled away in the night, southwards over the river.

159

The landlord's mouth opened and shut, opened and shut, but he knew no poetry with which to express his feelings. He was, after all, neither a theatrical man nor a poet.

SHAKESPEARE

The Theatre, London's first purpose-built permanent theatre was built by Richard Burbage's father James, in 1576. When the lease expired, Richard, Cuthbert, and the rest of the 'Chamberlain's Company' of actors, took its timbers to Southwark (maybe not in just the one night) and used them to build a new theatre. Several of them, including William Shakespeare, went into business together, sharing the profits. The building they put up was much the same octagonal shape as the Theatre had been—a wooden O.

This was the Globe Theatre, up and running. It made Shakespeare and his fellow shareholders rich men.

Richard Burbage played all the great Shakespearean roles—Hamlet, Othello, Lear, Macbeth, Richard III. But perhaps his greatest role was in creating the Globe Theatre, during the Golden Age of dramatic art.

In 1613 the Globe burned down during a performance of *Henry VIII*. It was rebuilt, but closed thirty years later when the Puritans suppressed the theatres as sinful. In 1997 it opened again, reconstructed in all its Elizabethan glory.

GUNPOWDER, TREASON AND PLOT

1604–1605

Guy Fawkes lit the fuse of the gunpowder and doubled back the way he had come. With an enormous thud, the charge went off, shattering the great slabs of the city wall into flying flint. Guido Fawkes had done it! His fellow troopers cheered, and the officers puffed out their cheeks in admiration at his cool, reckless courage.

That was at Calais. They made him a captain for his bravery at Calais. Everyone said there was no better explosives man in the Spanish army than Guido Fawkes of England.

He was still abroad eight years later when his old friend, Thomas Winter, came looking for him. He had a job for Guido—a job for a good explosives man. This time, however, Guido would be striking a blow for his religion—a blow for Catholicism, which England had suppressed with fire and sword for half a century. This time the target was Parliament.

The plot had already been hatched before Captain Fawkes joined it. In April conspirators met at the house of Robert Catesby, a tall, fair-haired man seething with indignation at the plight of English Catholics. King James (that worthless Scots popinjay) would gather, with all his lords and ministers, in the Lords' Chamber of the Palace of Westminster for the State Opening of Parliament. One explosion would put paid to the whole pack of them!

This was no rash, spur-of-the-moment piece of mischief. The conspirators gave themselves nine months to prepare. Thomas Percy, a white-haired, respected gentleman with influential friends, managed to secure a small house right alongside the palace. The cellar lay hard up against the cellars of the Lords' Chamber. All they had to do was tunnel through and lay the charge.

From May to December no one lived

in that house but Guido Fawkes—or rather 'John Johnson', for that was what he called himself.

December

All those days of waiting, doing nothing: for a man of action like Guido it was a torment. Then one December night, eleven men came to the door, darkly dressed, hats pulled down, spades and adzes and picks hidden under their clothes; also food and ale enough for a fortnight.

Down in the cellar they began to dig—not with great ringing, noisy blows, but with quiet gouging and grubbing and boring. They dug till their hands bled and their backs refused to straighten, but the tunnel progressed with ridiculous slowness.

'At this rate we shan't be through in time for the opening of Parliament!' Catesby fretted.

On 7 February it was announced by the town criers that the parliamentary session had been postponed indefinitely. The men in the cellars fell on each other's aching shoulders and laughed with relief. Time for a rest! Extra time for the tunnel to be finished! God must be on their side . . . but then they had known that all along.

That night, Guido Fawkes and Robert Keyes went across the river to a lock-up in Lambeth. It was dark, and no one saw the two men furtively transferring barrels to a nearby rowing boat. They had chosen a moonless night to row their gunpowder across the Thames to Westminster.

They dug by lantern light, those eleven desperate men, thinking to scratch their way through yards of solid rock. Then all of a sudden, in the middle of the day, came a rushing sound like water or an avalanche.

The diggers in the tunnel fell on their faces. Those nearest the cellar turned to run. What was it? Running feet? Were they found out? Or was the tunnel caving in on their heads?

It was neither. The rushing noise continued. 'John Johnson' ran outside into the street. There stood a wagon being filled with coal. The noise was of coal being shovelled out of a room *above* their tunnel—a room they had never even known existed! The coal merchant's vault must lie *directly below* the Lords' Chamber. They had never needed to dig a tunnel—only to secure that vault and pile their gunpowder there!

The tunnel was abandoned. God must truly be on their side—but then they had never doubted it.

Percy managed to rent the place. Spring and summer drifted by, with 'John Johnson' caretaker now of a coal-dusty vault. One by one, thirty-six kegs of gunpowder were transferred from their hiding place to the alcoves of the cellar.

October
In one week the hall above would be plush with ermine robes, glittering with coronets, crowded with Protestant statesmen.

Of course there would be Catholics, too. In among the elder statesmen would be good Catholic men, like Lord Monteagle. It upset the conspirators, of course it did. Catholics kill Catholics? Still, it could not be helped.

Perhaps someone thought it could. For Lord Monteagle received a letter—unsigned—advising him not to attend Parliament on 5 November, if he wanted to avoid an 'unseen blow'. Monteagle read and reread the letter, then sat tapping it against his lips, wondering what it could mean, what to do with it, who should see it . . .

4 November
It was time for Guido Fawkes, their explosives expert, to stack the kegs, lay the fuses and lie in wait to light them.

The other conspirators dispersed—some were already in the Midlands, ready to raise up the revolution in the wake of the bombing. Fawkes was cock-a-hoop. Sir Robert Cecil, Secretary of State, had ordered a search of the cellars, but his incompetent men had found nothing! The way was clear. The time was ripe.

Coal dust glittered like jet in the light from his candle. Guido made himself as comfortable as he could in the cold and clammy dark. His breathing was shallow, his heartbeat steady. This for Guido was a simple act of war. Below ground, he could not hear the church clocks striking midnight.

Tramp tramp tramp. There was the scrape of pikes against stone, a jangle of keys; dancing yellow lantern light sprang into the vault. So sure was Robert Cecil about the letter Monteagle had showed him that he had ordered a *second* search. This time his troopers saw the kegs at once. Then they saw, standing against the far wall, the dark figure of a tall man. He did not struggle as they bound his wrists.

They manhandled him all the way to the King's bedchamber, shouting questions in his face, punching and kicking him. But the man from the cellar gave only his name: 'John Johnson'.

5 November

Though the others fled, Sir Robert Cecil seemed to know exactly where to find them. Fawkes refused to name them, but they were tracked down anyway, within three days. They rushed out of doors, swords in hand, and three were gunned down: Catesby and Percy killed by a single bullet.

The gaolers broke Fawkes on the rack. It startled them how long he held out, but in the end, a man can be made to confess to anything on the rack.

He was the last to die. His fellow conspirators had all died traitors' deaths when Fawkes was led out to execution. But the crowd were still in good voice, taunting and jeering. 'Traitor! Coward! Murderer! Villain!

Devil!' Their hatred and disgust knew no bounds. They would savour his agonizing death: hanged, cut down alive, disembowelled, quartered, and only then beheaded. Guido could barely climb the ladder; the rack had crippled him. But shakily he reached the top, the hangman, the noose.

Whispering a prayer, he jumped from the ladder. His neck snapped. The crowd groaned. The villain had cheated them! He was already dead, and they had been robbed of an afternoon's entertainment.

Guido Fawkes, now referred to as Guy, was born Protestant, but converted to Catholicism after his widowed mother married a Catholic country gentleman. Full of religious zeal and a love of adventure, he left England in 1593 and went to fight in Catholic causes in Europe. He was thirty-five when he died.

In 1606 Parliament decreed that 5 November should be kept as a day of thanksgiving for their deliverance. But the burning of a guy on Bonfire Night is a later, Victorian addition to the festivities.